QUICKBOOKS

A Comprehensive Guide to Learning Quickbooks Concepts and Techniques for Beginners

BLAINE ROBERTSON

© Copyright 2019 - All rights reserved

No portion of this book may be reproduced- mechanically, electronically or by any other means, including photocopying without written permission from the author or the publisher.

Under no circumstances will any blame or legal responsibility be held against the publisher, or author, for any damages, reparation, or monetary loss due to the information contained within this book. Either directly or indirectly.

Legal Notice:
This book is copyright protected. This book is only for personal use. You cannot amend, distribute, sell, use, quote or paraphrase any part, or the content within this book, without the consent of the author or publisher.

Disclaimer Notice:
Please note the information contained within this document is for educational and entertainment purposes only. All effort has been executed to present accurate, up to date, and reliable, complete information. No warranties of any kind are declared or implied. Readers acknowledge that the author is not engaging in the rendering of legal, financial, medical or professional advice. The content within this book has been derived from various sources. Please consult a licensed professional before attempting any techniques outlined in this book.

By reading this document, the reader agrees that under no circumstances is the author responsible for any losses, direct or indirect, which are incurred as a result of the use of information contained within this document, including, but not limited to, — errors, omissions, or inaccuracies.

Table of Contents

Introduction 1

Chapter 1: Setting up QuickBooks 6

    Company File Creation 7

    Customizing QuickBooks for Your Business 10

    Familiarizing Yourself with the QuickBooks Homepage 14

    Setting up Customers, Vendors, and Jobs 17

    Creating Customers in QuickBooks 20

    Contact Information Entering 22

    Payment Information Input 23

    Sales Tax Information Specification 26

    Additional Customer Contact 28

    Job Creation in QuickBooks 29

    New Job Creation 30

Vendor Setup 31
Setting Up Payments 32
Setting up Sales Tax 34
Additional Info 35

Chapter 2: Sales And Income Managing 36
Creating And Sending Invoices 38
Receiving Payments 40
Creating And Sending Sales Receipts 43

Chapter 3: Bills And Expenses Managing 46
Creating And Sending Sales Receipts 49
Customize Sales Forms 50
Step by Step: Creating an Estimate 54
Step by Step: Create an Invoice from an Estimate 55
Step by Step: Create an Invoice for Unbilled Activity 56
Step by Step: Create an Invoice 57
Step by Step: Receive Payment 58
Step by Step: Entering Delayed Charge 59
Step by Step: Creating an Invoice from Quick Create 60
Step by Step: Recurring Transactions 60
Step by Step: Recurring Transaction List 61
Vendor Center 63
Step by Step: Creating a Bill 64
Step by Step: Entering Expense Type of Transaction 66
Step by Step: Paying Multiple Bills 67
Step by Step: Create a Check (write a check to pay a bill) 68

Step by Step: Print Checks in Batch...69
Step by Step: Using the Banking Center......................................70
Identify Additional Transactions Initiated Using The Quick Create Menu..75
Step by Step: Fill out a Single Time Activity 75
Step by Step: Fill out a Weekly Timesheet.................................76
Step by Step: Make a Bank Deposit 77
Entering Bills..79
Paying Bills...82

Chapter 4: Banking Transactions Managing 85
Banking Accounts Linking...87
Importing, Matching and Adding of Transactions 89
Bank Deposits Recording..91

Chapter 5: Business Credit Card Transaction Managing............96
Business Credit Card Reconciling 103

Chapter 6: Reporting..110
Profit and Loss/Balance Sheet 111
Step by Step: The Balance Sheet...117
Step by Step: Profit & Loss 119
Manage Accounts Receivable 122
Step by Step: Sales by Customer Summary 125
Step by Step: Sales by Customer Detail 126
Step by Step: Unbilled Charges 127
Manage Accounts Payable 128
Step by Step: A/P Aging Summary 129

Review Expenses And Purchases 129

Activity: Transaction List by Vendor................................... 130

Manage Payroll.. 131

Manage Sales Tax 131

Products And Inventory Managing 132

Step by Step: To run a Customer List 134

Step by Step: For Vendors... 135

Activity: Custom Reports... 136

Activity: Automatic Distribution... 137

Cash Flow Statement 139

Accounts Receivable and Payable Aging Report................... 140

Conclusion 142

QuickBooks Self-Employed... 144

QuickBooks Online 145

QuickBooks Desktop Products 147

QuickBooks Mac Desktop.. 149

QuickBooks Pro 150

QuickBooks Premiere.. 150

Frequently Asked Questions 153

Key Shortcuts... 159

References 162

Introduction

This guidebook is meant to help you with managing your business finances by guiding you through the basics of keeping appropriate records for your company using Quickbooks. It will help you with creating your company file in Quickbooks, setting up an accounts chart, depending on the field of work your company is engaged in, be it retail and E-commerce business (E-bay sellers, food trucks, coffee shops etc.), appointment-based business (doctor's office, driving school, dentist's office, etc.) or field service and professional businesses.

Whether you're a big business like Amazon, or an up-and-coming entrepreneur, QuickBooks is bound to increase the efficiency of your working process. As you already know, QuickBooks is a business running and accounting program. It allows you to handle a variety of different aspects of running your business.

From accounting to data entry, QuickBooks brings efficiency to your business process. No more hassling around with your accountant, no more posting data entry jobs on Amazon to find good underpaid workers.

The guide will show you how to keep better track of your bills in Quickbooks, as well as ensuring they are all paid on time. It will also help you go through tracking of your sales creating sale receipts and invoices for your customers. By regular and accurate updating of your record keeping information in Quickbooks, you will find it easier to make use of the multitude of financial reports that can be generated by Quickbooks for the analysis and better management of your business performance.

Introduction

QuickBooks Online is easy to use software designed for small business accounting. It lets your business track all your income, expenses, and inventory. It automatically tracks your GST and lets you manage your business payroll. QuickBooks Online Accountant offers a new way of supporting and managing your business and may change the way that you run your consulting, bookkeeping or accounting practice. QuickBooks Online Accountant lets you easily work with and manage your business using QuickBooks Online. QuickBooks Online is a cloud-based software.

- Secure - hosted securely by Intuit using bank-level security

- Accessibility - anywhere, anytime access using an internet connection.

- Data entry automation – get data into QuickBooks automatically using awesome features

- Unlimited Accountant Access – easy to connect with your accountant

- Mobile – businesses can access QuickBooks Online using their iOS or Android devices. No more being tied to the desktop, enter data when and where you are

- No Desktop files – no desktop files are required so no backups are required.

Seeing all these features, it's no surprise so many businesses are relying on digital technologies more and more. Compare QuickBooks to traditional accounting. With traditional accounting you're almost completely at the mercy of your accountant.

If your accountant makes a mistake, you'll have a rather hard time discovering it. On the other hand, QuickBooks lets you take the whole process into your hands. It is intuitive and easy to use, you don't need to go through college to be qualified to use it, in fact, this book is all you need!

If your company is big, you might want to have an accountant handle it anyways, but it also makes their job easier. QuickBooks is extremely easy to use for accountants, and it comes with the additional benefit of being easy to check for errors. This means that if there's an error, you'll be able to catch it quickly, possibly even before the payment is processed.

QuickBooks is also excellent for travelling entrepreneurs. You won't always have your PC or laptop with you, but QuickBooks will let you manage your business straight from your smartphone. QuickBooks eliminates any and all issues you might have had with the employees on your payroll.

QuickBooks also edges out against using on-site digital measures for your accounting. If you're using Excel sheets and Word documents, then you're at a high risk of being compromised. A

Introduction

simple fire or virus could end up annihilating all your files, incurring devastating loss. QuickBooks is cloud-based, meaning none of the files need to be stored on the devices you're using, so you're at no risk of being hacked. In fact, QuickBooks' security measures are at the level of an international bank.

With that being said, like with all advanced software, QuickBooks requires some training to learn. That's why this book is here, we'll guide you step by step through every nook and cranny of QuickBooks, making you an expert in less than 100 pages!

CHAPTER 1

Setting up QuickBooks

QuickBooks Online is easy to set up and get going. It is so simple that you can have a business file setup in less than 20 minutes. There are several important steps to follow to make sure that you are setting up business files efficiently and accurately.

The setup is optimized for speed and simplicity; however, it still requires some instruction. We'll dedicate this chapter to getting your QuickBooks business account up and running.

When you reach the end of this chapter, you should be able to:

- Set up a business file

- Set up basic settings

- Set up basic accounts

- Import list information Company File Setup

There are several important steps to set up your company file. Getting setup correctly will also help you and your Bookkeeper or Accountant stay compliant with GST and payroll taxes. In order to use QuickBooks Online, your business or you must subscribe to the software. Your business can subscribe by visiting intuit.com and signing up for a free trial. Your accountant can set up a business file from the QuickBooks Online Accountant.

Company File Creation

First thing's first: you need to create a company file, given that it's a place where you store all your company's financial records. You can either start from ground zero, by creating a new company file, or you can upload and convert records from another small business program. For those of you who are new to bookkeeping, there is always the option of using a file someone else created. For instance, if you had help from an accountant to start up your company, they might be able to help you once more by providing a QuickBooks company file that is already customized for your business, and in turn give you a head start.

If you don't have an accountant, worry not, we'll guide you through setting everything up, so you won't ever need one. Luckily, QuickBooks is rather simple to use, and setting up a business file isn't exactly rocket science.

At the beginning of this chapter we will explain how to start up your QuickBooks. Further, if you are starting your company file from scratch, we will guide you through the QuickBooks setup dialog box, as well as the Easy Step Interview to get you running (and to see what chapters besides this one help you to get the job done). On the other hand, if you are moving from another program, we will try to make the transition ride the least bumpy. Furthermore, we will go through opening of the company file, updating it to the latest version of QuickBooks, and basic company info modification.

- Start with visiting the QuickBooks site https://quickbooks.intuit.com, then signing in with your QuickBooks Online account. Once the site is opened, select the ''Create New Company" option, which can also be found in the "File" menu on the toolbar.

- Choose the "Start Interview" option and begin answering the interview questions.

- Enter your company information: You aren't required to fill in anything except the company name, but for the purpose of saving time and making things easier later on, you should fill in all the required information.

- Selecting your business industry should be the next step. By selecting your business industry type, QuickBooks will customize its settings to better accommodate the needs of your company.

- Next, select your company organization type (sole proprietorship, partnership, corporation, etc.). Correct selection of your company organization type will furthermore facilitate tax preparation later on.

- Select the first month of the annual accounting period. January is the usual starting month of the annual accounting period, but this can be modified to your company's preference.

- Set up the administrator's password. This is especially important if any other person except you has access to your computer or the company file so that only you will be privy to the full QuickBooks company file. Select "Next", then specify where do you want the company file to be saved

Customizing QuickBooks for Your Business

The QuickBooks Home page is laid out like the workflow you follow when you're bookkeeping, so it acts like a roadmap to many of the accounting tasks you perform. Shortcuts to other helpful QuickBooks features are sprinkled throughout the program's left icon bar; top icon bar; and Vendor, Customer, and Employee Centers. But your business isn't like anyone else's. Let's say you run a strictly cash-sales business, you couldn't care less about customer lists and invoices; making deposits, though, is a daily event. Fortunately, you don't have to accept QuickBooks' initial take on convenience. The Home page and the icon bars come stocked with a set of popular shortcuts, but you can add, remove, rearrange, and otherwise edit which features appear there. You can also add your favorite features, windows, and reports to the Favorites menu. This chapter covers all your options.

In addition to tweaking QuickBooks' layout, you can also customize the program's forms. QuickBooks helps you get up and running with built-in business form templates. They'll do if you have to blast out some invoices. But when you finally find a few spare minutes, you can create templates that show the information you want, formatted the way you want, and laid out to work with your letterhead. You can even create as many versions as you want. For example, you can make one invoice template to print on your letterhead and another for creating electronic invoices to the email that includes your logo, company name, and address.

This chapter describes the most efficient ways to create forms: using QuickBooks' form designs or built-in templates as a basis for your own.) Further down in this guide you can learn how to fine-tune forms with advanced customization techniques and even create templates from scratch.

- Further answer the Easy Step Interview Questions to customize Quickbooks for your company.

- If your company deals only in selling products, select "Products only". If you provide services in addition to selling products, "Both products and services" should be selected.

- Specify whether you sell products and/or services online.

- Select whether you charge sales tax.

- If you provide custom work or other services for which you wish QuickBooks to create estimates, select "Yes".

- If you take customer orders and want Quickbooks to track them, select "Yes".

- If you wish to use sales receipts, select "Yes".

- If you would like to be able to send and create billing statements, select "Yes".

- If you want to perform partial billing for payment, select "Yes" to use progress invoicing.

- Select "Yes" if you wish to keep track of the bills owed and receive reminders for when they are due.

- If you print checks or accept credit cards, select the appropriate answer.

- Select the preferred response for Inventory tracking.

- Select "Yes" if your company has more employees. Also, if tracking time spent on projects done by you or your employees, select "Yes".

- If your businesses involve multiple currencies, select the appropriate response.

- Using accounts in QuickBooks: to set up your accounts you need to know the date you would like to start from and how would you like to organize your income and expenses.

- Next, select a date to begin covering your finances. A reminder, whatever date you choose, all business activity that has occurred since that date must be entered. For this reason, it is simpler and more effective to choose a more recent date from which to begin tracking your finances with QuickBooks.

- Enter the appropriate bank accounts information, including the last bank statement ending date and balance

QuickBooks recommends a set of income and expense accounts based on the industry selection you made earlier in the interview. However, you can review these account selections and select or deselect any accounts to better reflect your business. Modifications or additions to your accounts chart or any part of the Easy Step Interview can be done at any time after the creation of your company file.

Familiarizing Yourself with the QuickBooks Homepage

Because you've got more than enough work to do with the running of your business, so you don't want bookkeeping to take any more time than necessary. QuickBooks' left icon bar and top icon bar both offer shortcuts to your favorite features. Each icon bar has its pros and cons, so you must decide which one you prefer (or you can turn them off completely). This chapter shows you how to access QuickBooks' features from the menu bar and icon bars. During a rousing bookkeeping session, you might find yourself with more than one QuickBooks window open simultaneously. In this chapter, you learn how to work with all the windows you open. If you prefer to focus on one task, you can tell QuickBooks to display only one window at a time.

As its name implies, Supermax view supersizes a window for you to see more info without scrolling. You'll learn lots of window tricks in this chapter. Another way to get your accounting done quickly and efficiently is by accessing features via the QuickBooks Home page. The page not only provides a visual roadmap of the bookkeeping tasks you perform regularly, but it also gives you quick access to tasks and information related to vendors, customers, and employees, along with the features and overall financial info you use most often. Click an icon, and the corresponding window or dialog box appears, such as Chart of Accounts, Item List, Write Checks, or everyone's favorite—Make Deposits. This chapter explains how to use the workflow icons on the Home page, as well as the Vendor, Customer, and Employees Centers that open when you click the corresponding buttons in the Home page's panels. You'll also see how to review your company's finances in the Company Snapshot window

The QuickBooks homepage is divided into several groups that are well-organized and connected with workflow arrows that will help you manage and perform business tasks better, faster and easier.

Vendors: The vendor area on the workflow diagram and the vendor center accessible on the toolbar help you to keep track of your purchases from various vendors, as well as categorize your expenses. Here you can create and edit your vendor list, make purchase orders, and enter and pay bills for your business. The vendor center gives you a complete picture of where your money is going. From one screen, you can see all your vendors and exactly what you owe them. Click on a vendor's name to view an entire history with that vendor. You no longer need to run separate reports to see exactly how much business you are doing with each individual vendor. Also, you can sort your bills by the due date so that you can stay on top of your finances. If you need to talk to a vendor, click on the vendor name to see all the contact information. If a vendor calls you to follow up on a late payment, you can look up the bill quickly and see the check number and when you paid it.

Customers: The Customer area and center will help you to manage any and all sales to customers. It also allows you to create estimates and invoices, track accounts and create statements, as well as receiving payments and creating sales receipts. The customers center is a lens for all your customer information. Without having to sift through multiple screens, you can view a list of all your customers and see pertinent information for each of them. Click on a customer's name and you immediately see all the activity you have had with them as well as their contact information (phone number, fax number, and payment terms)

Employees: Indicating in your Easy Step Interview that you have employees will cause an employee center to be created in order to better and easier manage your employees. The employees center lets you see exactly what you are paying each employee. Click on an employee's name to view that person's payroll history. If you need to get in touch with an employee, their contact information is right in front of you.

Company: The Company area of the workflow diagram will allow you to manage lists including your chart of accounts as well as items and service lists.

Banking: The Banking area helps you to record any deposits and write and print checks associated with any one of your bank accounts.

The specific icons appearing on the homepage depend upon your answers in the Easy Step Interview. Presuming you indicated that you would like to create an estimate in QuickBooks, an "Estimates" icon will appear in the Customers area, otherwise, the "Estimates" icon will not show. If you wish to change any of the settings created in the Easy Step Interview, select Edit → Preferences from the toolbar and you can change your personal or company preferences at any desired time.

Setting up Customers, Vendors, and Jobs

Maybe you enjoy parading through your sales department trumpeting, "We aren't getting anywhere until someone sold something! "It is quite possible for you to cite that maxim in your accounting department as well.

It doesn't matter whether you sell products or provide services, bagging the first sale with a new customer creates an avalanche of possible actions, including, but not limited to making a new customer entry, creating a job for the work and the much expected and desired goal that is invoicing (delivering a bill for the service provided or goods sold, which states how much the customer owes to you) your customer for the purpose of collecting income. The parties to which you provide services or sell products go by a myriad of names: shoppers, clients, consumers, members, etc. In the QuickBooks dictionary, there is only one word that fits the person, party or group of people who buy goods or services from you, and the word is the customer. In QuickBooks, a customer represents a documentation of information concerning your in-vivo customer. Quickbooks uses the information you entered about your customers, and with it completes sales forms as well as invoices with your client's names, payment terms, address, and other general information.

Real-world customers the key to your success, though are the customers in QuickBooks really that necessary? Despite you running a, let's say, primary cash business, cataloguing your customers in Quickbooks isn't such a bad idea. For instance, creating QuickBooks records for the recurring customers at your store cuts your time necessary to fill out their information on each new sale by doing it automatically. Furthermore, if your business is project-oriented, you can assign a job for each project you start for a customer in QuickBooks. For QuickBooks, a project is each job you signed (or was begged to sign) to perform for a customer—repairing a yacht, creating a billboard ad, anything really. Let's say you are an electrician, and you do work for a general contractor on a regular basis.

You might set up several jobs, one for Setting Up Customers, Jobs, and Vendors, for each place you do work at: Scott estate, Hammond estate, and Julliard estate. Then you can see and track expenses and income by job and assess the profitability for each and every one. Although, if your business doesn't handle jobs, there is no need for you to set them up in QuickBooks. For instance, record stores sell record, not services or projects. If your business doesn't do jobs, you can just create customers in QuickBooks and simply continue to invoice them, or even filling out sales receipts for their purchases. Although, before you begin receiving payments, you will need to get busy with the vendors and pay up for their products and/or services. The Internet service provider, your marketing manager, and the hardware store that sells you the equipment all fall into the category of vendors. Information required to be filled out isn't that much different from that of the customers.

Deeper into this guide you will learn how to create customers, vendors, and jobs in QuickBooks. You will also learn how to apply the program's customer, vendor, and job fields for your business. And you'll learn how to manage the customer, job, and vendor records you create in QuickBooks.

Creating Customers in QuickBooks

Unfortunately, your first task is to convince would-be customers to work with your company. After you've worked around that obstacle, it's clear sailing to creating customers in QuickBooks. More than one way to create a customer record is available in this:

1. Using QuickBooks Setup. After starting this app, you can easily use the Setup dialogue box to get customer information, along with the employee and vendor info. You can also get the info via email, or simply paste it from Excel. If you want to input more records to this, just go back to Setup.

2. One by one. It is advisable to use the New Customer option when you want to create customers. Unfortunately, sometimes you don't have the time to create them one by one, so it is also possible to do in bulk without closing the tab.

Customers can also be inserted into the system in bulk. The Add/Edit Multiple List Entries are useful because they let you move data from any Excel-like software and copy information from customers onto others. The Customer Center is a gathering place for jobs and customers alike: viewing, creation, and modification of the records, as well as transaction creation. The Customer Center can be opened in four simple ways:

1. Pressing CTRL+J while the app is open

2. Pressing "Customers" in the header of the Customers tab of the QuickBooks homepage.

3. Open the menu, press on Customers, then go to the Customer Center.

4. The icon bar contains a "Customers" option, press there.

Now for a quick and easy method of creating a single customer in QuickBooks:

1. Use the toolbar contained in the Customer Center to create a new customer with their job.

2. In the Customer Name field, type a code or a unique name, followed by the naming convention you've chosen. Everything else you can ignore; this is the only field that is mandatory to fill in.

3. To archive the said customer's record and exit the New Customer window, select OK. To discard any entries and changes you made, select Cancel.

To create a job for a customer, close the New Customer window and open the New Job window. It's a lot faster to create all your customers first and then add the jobs for each one. To help you find what you want to fill out, the New Customer and Edit customer tabs are separated into sections. Both the contact and the address info are found within the 1st section, the Address info. Any fields that are related to payments can be found on the Payment Setting tab. The next tab, Sales Tax Settings, can be completely skipped in the case that your business doesn't sell taxable goods. Next, Additional Info tab, which used to be a jumble of different types of fields, now has a couple of miscellaneous fields, like sales rep, customer type, and custom fields you've created. The following few sections will guide you through each tab and its respective fields.

Contact Information Entering

In the case you intend to bill your customers, send them products, or to just check in on them, you will need to have the address and contact information. You can write this down in the New Customer's Address info tab. A quick advice on how to fill this tab:

Company Name - This is where you put a way for the program to refer to the customer, be it a name or a nickname. Note, however, that the way you call them here is how they'll be referred to on invoices and other documents you do via this app. After you're done QuickBooks will automatically insert that name into the "Bill To" section.

Contact - This is the place where you enter the primary contact's name, as well as what you wish to refer to them with, for the purpose of addressing letters, invoices and other communication between companies. Please note that QuickBooks copies everything you entered here into Invoice/Bill To field. This will also let you input the Job's title.

Invoice/Bill To - This is where you'll place the address you wish to show on your invoices. If you want to change it, there's the Edit button, as well as other options which will help you specify your street, postal code, street address and other basic information. Naturally, QuickBooks also supports copy-pasting this from anywhere else.

Ship To - If you won't be shipping anything to your customer, then there's no need to fill this out. However, if you are shipping things, then first you'll need to check if the shipping and billing address are the same. If they are, you'll just need to press Copy and you're done with it. If they aren't, you'll need to add the shipping address manually.

Payment Information Input

The Payment Settings window is there to display how much you're owed, as well as how much you want to extend the customer's credit. In these fields, you'll need to input the customer's payment information such as:

Account Number. - In QuickBooks, account numbers are entirely optional. Big accounting programs usually assign specific numbers to customer records, which in turn speeds up the process of locating them. The Customer Number field is an identifier, so you should probably keep it the same as any of your other business apps.

Terms of Payment - This section belongs to the terms you and your customer have agreed to follow. It is used by the program for both your payment terms towards your customers, as well the terms you've agreed to with your vendors. This also includes the most used methods, which can help if you're just trying to get your business off the ground and don't know much about it. You can also define your own payment terms, which will make it so you don't need to insert them every time you use QuickBooks to send an invoice.

Preferred Delivery Method - You can choose from e-mail, mail or none to establish a method of delivery of information that your customer prefers. If you select E-mail, QuickBooks will automatically activate the e-mail check box whenever you create forms for this specific customer. The Mailing method displays QuickBooks Billing Solutions, an add-on QuickBooks service for mailing invoices, though additional billings may apply. If you prefer to print out information, and then send it the old-fashioned way, you should select None.

Preferred Payment Method - This allows you to choose the preferred payment method of your customer. The drop-down list includes but is not limited to the few most frequent methods, such as check, cash, or credit card, though you can add others if you desire so. The payment method specified will appear automatically when you select this customer in any of your future endeavors, useful for repeat clients. If a customer wants to pay with a method different than the one you specified here, simply select said method in the Receive Payments window.

Credit card information - Concerning credit card payments, you can specify all relevant information such as the name on the card, billing address, postal code, and the expiration that can all be specified. It should be brought to attention that you can only enter one credit card number for one customer.

Credit Limit - Here you can specify the amount of credit you're willing to extend for the customer in question. If you do so, then QuickBooks will warn you whenever an invoice, or an order exceeds the amount of credit limit you specified, but it will not stop you from going through with the order, that is entirely up to you. If you don't intend to go through with the credit limitation, it might be best that you skip entering values in this field.

Price Level - Most businesses will have different price levels for different customers. A good example of this is how not everyone pays the same for airline tickets. QuickBooks will let you insert discounts and markups to process for these transactions. You can have multiple pricing levels and name them however you'd like. This will let you be much more organized when it comes to giving out discounts or markups. Quickbooks also makes it easy to apply these for any purchases a given customer makes.

Add Online Payment Link to Invoices - Online payment links on invoices allow customers to pay you through the Intuit Payment Network either by making a payment directly from their bank accounts into yours or by credit card. (The fees you pay for this service vary based on how the customers pay). However, setting up this feature requires a couple of steps. First, be sure to sign up for the Intuit Payment Network service. If you don't sign up and your customers click an online payment link, they'll see a message telling them that you haven't signed up for the service yet. There's a section called Payment settings, which you can use to instruct QuickBooks which online payment option to use for the customer. "Follow Company Default" applies the setting that you selected in QuickBooks' preferences. Choosing "Always ON (bank only)" means the customer can pay only through a bank account regardless of your company preference. With "Always ON (bank or credit card)," the customer can pay by bank account or credit card. "Always OFF for this customer" means QuickBooks doesn't display the online payment link on this customer's invoices.

Sales Tax Information Specification

Now, the Sales Tax window will pop up regardless of whether you've turner Quickbooks Sales Tax on or not, which can be a bit annoying to some users. While that's true, if you don't have it turned on, it'll be practically useless. All the fields in the window will be covered with a monotone grey, signaling they aren't to be

Setting up QuickBooks

used. Now if you do pay sales tax, you'll want to choose the Tax option in the Tax Code tab and pick the rate.

There's also a variety of ways to customize your customers. The following will show you the fields that can be filled in, and a few simple ways the can be used:

- Customer Type. You can categorize the customers by type, which can ease communication that is customized for each type, or to determine which types pay off the most. After you've set up customer types, you can categorize a customer by choosing from this list, it will display the entries from your Customer Type List.

- Rep. Adding a name in this field links a sales representative to a customer, which can aid you with tracking of the results of the sales reps. To make sure your customers receive the best customer service, it is recommended to assign a customer service representative to every customer, as to keep them in constant communication with your company regarding all your services. When you start creating a Rep entry, you can use the existing names in the Vendor, Employee, or Other names list, or, if you wish so, add a new name to use as a rep.

- Custom Fields. QuickBooks provides up to 15 custom fields, which you can be used to enter key information for which QuickBooks doesn't provide. Given that custom fields do not have drop-down list, all your entries need to be entered consistently.

Additional Customer Contact

While you're making a customer file, you can determine information about a single contact in the Address Info tab in the New Customer window. You can specify which jobs those contacts perform. Furthermore, all these contacts are also editable, and you're able to delete them as you see fit, this is most useful in case the people you've got saved are in the process of or have already changed their job.

After selecting a customer, you'll get to see the contact information for them, as well as have the option to simply add even more contacts to their record. This can be accomplished by clicking on Manage Contacts in the lower-right corner and selecting Add New. After that, all you need to do is finish the info boxes and whatever other additions you wanted to introduce. When you're done with it, simply click Save and Close and QuickBooks will exit the window.

Job Creation in QuickBooks

If you are involved in project-based work, you are aware that every job has a starting point and an ending one. Whether you build custom housing or surveillance systems, QuickBooks' job-tracking features can be used for financial performance analysis by project.

Let's say you wish to know if you're earning money on the suburban estate building, or on the remodeling low-income estates, in addition to the percentages pertaining to your success/fail ratio. If you use QuickBooks for this, It'll easily and smoothly estimate the financials around it, it'll be almost like having an accountant! Jobs and customers are inseparable from each other in the program, so you'll want to keep a close eye on both. A job will always stay with a customer. If you tried making your job before you've finished creating a customer, a message box will pop out notifying you that first you need to make a simple customer file in order to create a job. Thankfully there are two tabs for both creating and editing customers, both contain tabs for the customer information, as well as job information. So, effectively, whenever you create a customer, you automatically create one job with it, although you can add more jobs later on, if it is necessary. The following section will show you how to do just that.

New Job Creation

As it was mentioned before, in order to create a job, you must create a customer first. When you are done with the creation of the customer, complete these simple steps in order to add a job to a customer's record:

- Under the Customer Center's Customers & Jobs tab, right-click the customer for which you wish to create a job, next select Add Job in the shortcut menu. As well, you can select the New Customer & Job tab->New Job. In both cases, a New Job window will open.

- In the Job Name box, enter a name for the desired job. Choose it well, as it will appear on invoices and/or other customer documents. Up to 41 characters can be typed in this box. Job name should be as short and as descriptive as possible both for you and your customer. QuickBooks will fill in the rest of the job fields using the information you entered for the customer for which the job is created. You will only need to manually edit the fields on the Payment settings, Address Info, and Additional Info. Let's say that the address for the material shipping for the job differs from the customer's, you will then be required to fill out the corresponding fields.

- If you wish to provide further information about the position, select the Job Info tab and enter values in the proper areas. If you're adding sorts of jobs, you can cross-reference these with other jobs that share characteristics. This also doesn't change based on which customer gave you the position. If you input information in the Job Status section, it's going to give you a recap of exactly what's happening in the Customer Center. If deadlines are a concern for you, you can estimate the dates for the job, and simply insert those in the appropriate area.

- Once you're done with that, simply press OK, QuickBooks will then save the job and close the window.

Vendor Setup

In order to make a new vendor entry through the Vendor Center, press CTRL and N at the same time. You can also do this through the menu bar, however, the shortcut streamlines things. Now, most of the fields you will find are quite similar to the customer creation field. This should make the process quite a bit easier, for example the Vendor Name and Customer Name fields work the exact same way, making it a lot easier to navigate through. Similarly, QuickBooks advises leaving the Opening Balance field without an entry, and instead building the Vendor Balance by inputting invoices and payments. This can prove to be quite helpful, especially when the vendor and the customer are the same people, just for different products.

Now, if you're printing off your bills and all the sheets you need to pay them, you'll have to place some contact and address info here, so that QuickBooks knows where to send them. These fields are quite obviously quite similar to the corresponding customer fields, they are also filled the exact same way, so once you've mastered that feel free to move onto payments.

Setting Up Payments

Payments are in the Payment Settings section, and they, while rather easy to fill, are also integral, so we'll walk you through it, nonetheless.

- The Account Number is pretty much the same as the customer account number section. Naturally, in this case it's reversed, and the vendors give your company a number, rather than vice-versa. After the vendor gives you your number, you just need to input it here. Obviously, you should keep this number secure and close to you. This is because there's a lot of malpractice that can be done with it, and it serves as easy proof in case of trouble.

- As with before, you'll be selecting the payment terms under which you and the vendor will operate. Once you've got a deal with your vendor, simply input it here, quite similar to the customer settings.

- Now when it comes to the way your name will be printed on the checks, QuickBooks will auto-fill it with the info you already entered. You can change it; however, it generally isn't advised.

- Again, same as the customer side, you want to input the credit limit. This is the amount of credit that a vendor is willing to give you. You simply input however much that is, and QuickBooks will notify you every time you're trying to get past this pre-set limit. This can be quite useful as it lets you always keep your credit limit in mind.

- The Billing Rate Level is again, same as the customer side of things just inversed. If you have any kind of special discount with a vendor, this will help you set it up. Instead of tediously going through all your numbers and dropping them by say, 10%, you can simply insert this in QuickBooks, and it'll do it for you. It also works for billing employees, so if you bill them by seniority you could have a category for every year they've worked and how much of a raise they've accrued so far. This is one of the most underrated capabilities of QuickBooks and you'd do best to use it to the fullest

Setting up Sales Tax

In the Tax Settings tab, QuickBooks has two fields. They are as follows:

1. Vendor ID. You are only required to put in the vendor's social security number or the employer's identification no, EIN for short, if you intend to do a 1099 form for the said vendor.

2. Vendor suitable for 1099 form. Mark this checkbox if you intend to create a 1099 for this vendor.

While writing a check, for upcoming payments, or simply to check out the changes in the vendor credit card, mark the account to which you want to give the payment. The Vendor options, including creation and editing enable QuickBooks to know which accounts you usually use. The easiest way to solve the hassle of expense accounts is to simply allow QuickBooks to access the previous monetary transactions you've made. This way, whenever you record a bill, credit card changes or a check for someone, QuickBooks will create a brand-new bill by using the total amount and the accounts you selected on the previous transaction.

Additional Info

With all the New Vendor window's tabs, the Additional Info tab is rather sparse, which is probably why it's the last tab in the list. Here are its fields and what you can do with them:

- To enable you to categorize vendors, QuickBooks has a useful function called the Vendor Type, which will let you sort out vendors. As an example, if you give all agencies you pay taxes to the same tax type, you'll be having a much easier time reporting your taxes.

- Now, if you're trying to get to different information, you'll have to use the custom setting, which will let you set everything manually. You are eligible to add seven more custom fields.

CHAPTER 2

Sales And Income Managing

Notifying your customers of the amount they owe you, as well as payment deadlines is an important step in accounting. After all, if money isn't flowing into your organization from outside sources, eventually you'll close shop and close your QuickBooks company file for the last time.

Although businesses use several different sales forms to bill customers, the invoice is the most popular, and, unsurprisingly, customer billing is often called invoicing. This chapter begins by explaining the differences between invoices, statements, and sales receipts—each of which is a way of billing customers in QuickBooks—and when each is most appropriate. After that, you'll learn how to fill in invoice forms in QuickBooks, whether you're invoicing for services, products, or both. If you send invoices for the same items to many of your customers (and don't use the program's multiple currencies feature), QuickBooks' batch invoice feature can help: You select the customers, add the items you want on the invoices, and the program creates all the invoices for you.

If you track billable hours and reimbursable expenses with QuickBooks, you can also have the program chuck those charges into the invoices you create.

Finally, you'll find out how to handle a few special billing situations, like creating invoices when the products you sell are on backorder. You'll also learn how to create estimates for jobs and then use them to generate invoices as you perform the work. And, since you occasionally have to give money back to customers (like when they return the lime-green polyester leisure suits that suddenly went out of style), you'll learn how to assign a credit to a customer's account, which you can then deduct from an existing invoice, refund by cutting a refund check, or apply to the customer's next invoice.

Creating And Sending Invoices

An invoice is a form you use to charge customers for everything, ranging from an app to a loaf of bread that they purchase from you. When your customers do not pay you in full at the time you provide your service or product, or when they pay in advance, you need to track how much they owe you. You can use an invoice to help you keep track of what your customers owe you (or your accounts receivable). Invoices list all the details about the sale, including the services you are providing or the products you are selling (your items). Invoices also show the quantity and price or rate of each item. If you need to make automatic adjustments to prices (for example, discounts or markups), invoices will work for you.

- Depending on which edition of QuickBooks you use, you have up to three features for creating invoices:

- Create Invoices can handle everything you throw at it: services, products, billable time, and billable expenses. It's available in QuickBooks Pro and higher.

- Create Batch Invoices lets you select all the customers to which you want to send the same invoice (that is, the same items and the same amounts). If you send the same invoice to the same customers all the time, you can set up a billing group for those customers and, from then on, simply choose the group. After you create the invoice, you can print or email it to the customers in the list. This feature is available in QuickBooks Pro and higher, as long as you don't use multiple currencies.

- Invoice for Time & Expenses, available only in QuickBooks Premier and Enterprise editions, can do everything that the Create Invoices feature can do, but it's a real time-saver when you invoice for billable time and expenses. You specify a date range and QuickBooks shows you all the customers who have billable time and expenses during that period. When you choose a customer or job and tell the program to create an invoice, it opens the Create Invoices window, fills in the usual fields, and fills the invoice table with the customer's billable time and expenses. Once you're in the Create Invoices window, you can add any other items you want, like products you sold or discounts you're offering. This feature also lets you create batch invoices for time and expenses.

- Invoices inform your customers about every bit of information they need to know about what they purchased and what they owe you. If you created customers and jobs with settings such as payment terms, tax item, and sales rep, as soon as you choose a customer and job in the Create Invoices window's Customer: Job field, QuickBooks fills in many of the fields for you.

Receiving Payments

In between performing work, invoicing customers, and collecting payments, you should keep track of who owes you how much (known as Accounts Receivable) and when the money is due. Sure, you can tack on finance charges to light a fire under your customers' accounting departments, but such charges are rarely enough to make up for the time and effort you spend collecting overdue payments. Far preferable are customers who pay on time without reminders, gentle or otherwise. Because companies need money to keep things running, you'll have to spend some time keeping track of your Accounts Receivable and the payments that come in. In this chapter, you'll learn the ins and outs of tracking what customers owe, receiving payments from them, and dinging them if they don't pay on time. You'll get up to speed on Income Tracker, a handy dashboard that shows estimates you've created, how much customers owe—both overdue and not—and what's been paid in the past 30 days. QuickBooks' Collections Center can highlight customers with overdue or almost-due invoices, gather the info you need to collect what customers owe, and make it easy to send out reminders. In contrast to invoices, sales receipts are the simplest and most immediate sales forms in QuickBooks. When your customers pay in full at the time of the sale—at your retail store, for example—you can create a sale's receipt, so the customer has a record of the purchase and payment. At the same time, QuickBooks will send the money that you've gained straight into your account with almost any bank. (Sales receipts work only when customers pay in full, because that type of sales form can't handle previous customer payments and balances.) In this chapter, you'll learn how to create sales receipts for one sale at a time and to summarize a day's worth of merchandising.

When you receive money from a customer, you should record the transaction and mark the invoice as paid. When you receive a payment, the accounts receivable records are updated, and the payment is ready to be deposited into an account.

1. To receive a payment:

2. Go to the Customers menu and click Receive Payments.

3. Fill in the top portion of the form, including the customer's name, the payment amount, payment method, and the date on which the payment was received.

4. Check the column to the left of the invoice to which you want to apply the payment. You might be asked to decide how to apply the payment for one of the following scenarios:

5. The overpayment can become a credit or refund

6. Underpayment can be left as is or written off

7. The customer has unused credit to be applied

8. The customer has available discounts

9. Choose the appropriate selection and you should see your choices reflected in total amounts for selected invoices. If the customer has a discount or available credits, you can choose how to apply them.

10. Click "Save & Close" or "Save & New" if you have more customer payments to receive.

You can set a preference so that payments received either go to any account you've set up for funds that haven't been deposited automatically, or automatically get calculated and applied as you select invoices in the list. To set this preference, go to the Edit menu, click Preferences, and then click the Company Preferences tab in the Sales & Customers area

Creating And Sending Sales Receipts

A sales receipt is the form you use when you make a sale for which you receive full payment at the time of the sale. Sales receipts can include payments by cash, check, or credit card. When your customers pay in full at the time they receive your service or product, you do not need to track how much they owe you. However, you might want to record the sale, calculate its sales tax, or print a receipt for the sale. In these cases, you can create a sales receipt. Examples of businesses that commonly use sales receipts include beauty salons, pet groomers, dry cleaners, and restaurants. If you need to track how much a customer owes you or you do not receive full payment at the time of the transaction, do not use a sales receipt. Instead, create an invoice, as described previously in this chapter.

To enter a sales receipt:

1. Go to the Customers menu and click Enter Sales Receipts.

2. Fill in the top part of the form, including the Customer: Job, Date, and Payment Method.

3. Click the Template drop-down arrow and then click the sales receipt template you want to use.

4. In the bottom part of the form, enter the items purchased.

5. Save the transaction

You can also use a sales receipt to create a summary of sales income and sales tax owed. You can summarize daily or weekly sales on a sales receipt.

At any time, you can go to the customer center and see all your customers and those with balances listed at the left-hand side of the customer center. Above the customers list, you can select to view all customers or just those with open balances by selecting from the drop-down box under "Customers & Jobs." In the lower portion of the customer center you can see a list of all your transactions with customers including invoices, recorded deposits, sales receipts, etc. You can also select specific types of transactions and specific time periods using the drop-down boxes above the transactions list and the list will be modified to your specifications.

CHAPTER 3

Bills And Expenses Managing

Although most small business owners sift through the daily mail looking for envelopes containing checks, they usually find more containing bills. One frustrating aspect of running a business is that you often must pay for the items you sell before you can invoice your customers for the goods.

If you want your financial records to be right, you must tell QuickBooks about the expenses you've incurred. And, if you want your vendors to leave you alone, you have to pay the bills they send. Paying for expenses can take several forms, but QuickBooks is up to the challenge. This chapter explains your choices for paying bills (now or later) and describes how to enter bills and record your bill payments. If you pay right away, you'll learn how to write checks, use a debit or credit card, and pay with cash in QuickBooks, among other options. If you enter bills in QuickBooks for payment later, you'll learn what to do with the recurring ones, as well as reimbursable expenses and inventory. QuickBooks is happy to help you through every step of the process: entering bills you receive if you want to pay later, setting up bill payments, and even printing checks you can mail to vendors.

When to Pay Expenses When it comes to handling expenses, you can pay now or pay later; QuickBooks has features for both options. (You can choose to not pay bills, but QuickBooks can't help you with collection agencies or represent your company in bankruptcy court.) Here are the pros and cons of each approach:

- Pay now. If bills arrive about as often as meteor showers, go ahead and pay each one immediately so you're sure they're paid on time. In QuickBooks, paying right away means writing a check, entering a debit card transaction, entering a credit card charge, making an online payment, or using money from petty cash—all of which are described in this chapter. When you pay immediately, you don't have to enter a bill in QuickBooks; you can simply record the expense payment transaction.

- Pay later. If bills arrive as steadily as orders at the local coffee shop, you'll probably want to set aside time to pay them all at once when it won't interfere with delivering services or selling products. What's more, most companies don't pay bills until just before they're due—unless there's a good reason to (like an early payment discount). Setting up vendor bills for later payment is known as using Accounts Payable because you store the unpaid expenses in an Accounts Payable account.

In QuickBooks, entering bills for later payment delivers all the advantages of convenience and good cash management. You can tell the program when you want to pay bills—for instance, to take advantage of an early payment discount or the grace period that a vendor allows. Then you can go about your business without distraction, knowing that QuickBooks will let you know when bills are on deck for payment.

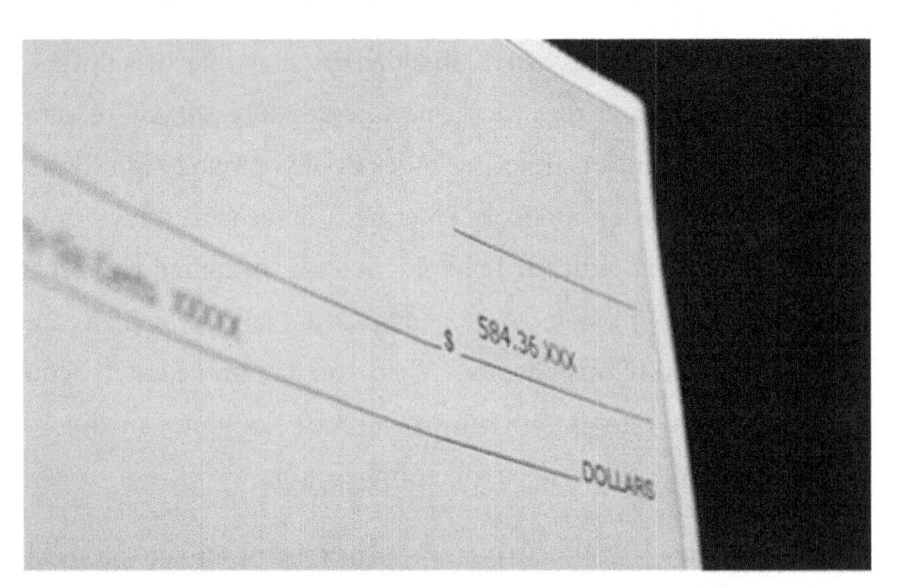

Creating And Sending Sales Receipts

Whenever you set up a new area of QuickBooks, you need to review the company settings related to that area. Before you go into the Company Settings, you need to make sure you understand the different types of sales and revenue transactions. Estimates – are non-posting transactions that allow you to provide your customers with information on what you think you are going to charge them. Think of it as a quote or a proposal Invoice – the sales transaction used when you want to allow the customer to pay on account.

An invoice will increase Accounts Receivable and increase income Payment – the type of transaction used to receive payment against an invoice. It decreases Accounts Receivable and increases either a bank account or Undeposited Funds Sales Receipt – this sales transaction is used when you receive payment at the time of sale. It increases income and increases either a bank account or Undeposited Funds Credit Memos – are used when a customer returns something or negotiates a lower price.

This creates a credit in Accounts Receivable that can be used against future invoices Refund Receipts – are also used when a customer returns something or negotiates a lower price, but, with a refund receipt, you are refunding their payment Delayed Charges and Credits – are available in Essentials and Plus only and are non-posting transactions that reflect potential revenue increase or decrease. They can be used on future transactions.

Company Settings

Click on the Gear icon to access the Company Settings. There are four tabs along the left-hand side to set the preferences as to how you want to use the company file. Sales has its own category, but there are also sales settings under the Advanced Settings.

Customize Sales Forms

The first setting under the Sales tab allows you to customize the sales forms. The customization applies to Invoices, Estimates and Sales Receipts. You can choose your style, including uploading your logo.

Click on the Header tab. This allows you to rename the title of your sales forms (i.e., change an estimate to a quote), as well as identify which fields you want to see in the Header section including three custom fields. The Columns tab allows you to identify which columns you want to see and put them in whatever order you want.

The Footer tab allows you to add a custom message as well as an additional footer on invoices. The More tab allows you to make further refinements. Make sure to look at billable time and expenses if you invoice based on time and expenses. When you invoice for time, you can include the employee name on the form as well as group activities by time period or type and have the groups subtotaled.

You can also show an account summary at the top of the form. This gives you the balance forward, the new invoice charges and the total due. Sales form content This allows you to set options such as preferred invoice terms and delivery method which can be changed on an actual sales form. It's setting defaults. You can also decide to add additional line items such as shipping, discounts or deposit fields. When you customized the forms previously, you had the ability to add three custom fields to the transactions.

That preference is turned on in the Sales form content and the fields can be set up here or on the Customization page. But please note here is where you indicate if you want the custom fields to be internal, public or both. Products and Services In this area, you identify if you want to show the Product/Service column on sales forms so that the dropdown list of the Products and Services List is available. Here also is where you turn on the preference of tracking inventory. Inventory is only available in QuickBooks Online Plus. Other sales settings The Messages setting allows you to create default email text when emailing sales forms as well as a default message on the form itself. Online Delivery settings relate to emailing your forms and what you want the customer to see. There are options of sending as plain text, HTML or using Online invoice.

There are a couple of preferences to choose from regarding statements. Advanced settings Make sure to look under the Automation section of the Advanced settings. Pre-fill forms are asking you if you want QuickBooks to copy over the same information form the last transaction using the same customer. If you turn on the preference to automatically apply credits, QuickBooks will apply any available credits to the next invoice. Beware of turning this (or any other automation) preference on.

It may be that your client doesn't want to apply the credit to the next invoice — but apply it to some future invoice. You can turn on a preference to have QuickBooks automatically invoice unbilled activity. If you turn this on, you will receive a notification in the Activities feed on the Home page. If you want to invoice from an estimate, you need to turn on the preference to copy estimates to invoices. You then have a choice to copy only for accepted estimates or pending and accepted estimates. You really must know your client and be confident that turning on the Automation preferences makes sense for them. If you find that a client is having problems with Accounts Receivable, check these settings.

Recognize Alternative Entry Points For Entering Sales Transactions

Customer Center

The Customer Center, accessed by selecting Customers in the left navigation bar, is a dashboard for adding, editing and reviewing customers with which your client QuickBooks Online company does business. The list of Customers can be printed or exported, and it can be sorted by various parameters or filtered. Beside each Customer listing is a drop-down box from which to create transactions such as invoices or estimates, or to send a reminder of a balance owing or print or send a statement. In addition, batch actions can be performed for the entire list: sending or printing statements and sending emails directly from within QuickBooks Online. These emails can use your choice of web-based email or email client. Entering Transactions from the Customer Center

Step: Creating an Estimate

There are several ways to create an Estimate in QuickBooks Online. To create an Estimate from the Customer Center, follow these steps:

1. Select Customers from the left navigation bar.

2. If necessary, select Clear Filter/View All above the Money Bar to produce a full listing of Customers.

3. Select the drop-down box in the far-right column for the desired customer -> Create Estimate.

4. Complete the on-screen estimate for the desired customer, with the desired date, Products and Services of your choosing, the quantity, description (override the description if you want) and rate (override the rate if you like) of each, the sales tax (check the box for tax for specific items and then select the sales tax to be applied below in the dropdown box).

5. Complete any other desired fields such as the Discount and the Message to the Customer.

6. Select Save and close or (by clicking on the drop-down box next to Save and Close) select Save and New.

Step by Step: Create an Invoice from an Estimate

To create an Invoice from the Estimate you just created, the easiest way of finding that Estimate is to do so from the Money Bar in the Customer Center.

1. Select Customers from the left navigation bar.

2. Click on the Estimates rectangle in the far-left section of the Money Bar. (This creates a listing of open Estimates.)

3. Locate Cool Cars, for which you created that Estimate and click on 1 open estimate.

4. In the Transactions listing that appears, find the estimate you want to turn into an invoice, then select Start invoice at the far right.

5. Make changes to the already-populated invoice as required.

6. Select Save and close or (by clicking on the drop-down box next to Save and Close) select Save and New.

A quick heads-up: If you do not want to invoice for the whole amount of the estimate, you can change the quantity or line items on the invoice. However, QuickBooks still considers the estimate fully invoiced. There is no progress invoicing in QuickBooks Online.

Step by Step: Create an Invoice for Unbilled Activity

You can also easily create invoices for any unbilled activity.

1. Select Customers from the left navigation bar.

2. Click on the Unbilled Activity rectangle in the left section of the Money Bar. (This creates a listing of any unbilled activity.)

3. Note that you can see a listing of unbilled activity and click on Start Invoice from here or click to see the unbilled activity. Click on Unbilled activity for the customer for which you wish to see the unbilled activity.

4. Click on Start Invoice.

5. Heads-up: If you have multiple activities listed here, you can create a separate invoice for each activity. If you want to create one invoice for all unbilled activities, do it from the Customer Center itself.

6. Add any additional charges, sales tax or discounts and Save and close.

7. Entering Transactions from the Sales Transactions page (Sales Center)

Step by Step: Create an Invoice

1. Click on Sales under Transactions on the Navigation bar

2. This opens the Sales Transactions or Sales Center. Under the Actions column, there are suggested next steps. You can filter the Money Bar here the same way you can in the Customer Center. You can also create New Transactions at the top right hand of the screen. Click on Invoice

3. Create a new invoice for the desired customer. When you enter the customer name, QuickBooks opens a drawer on the right side that shows you time or expense activities that have been marked Billable. You can easily add them to the invoice. The difference between creating the invoice from here and creating it from the Action column for that customer or activity is that here you have a choice of what you are adding where if you create an invoice from the Action column it automatically puts the unbilled activity on the invoice.

4. Invoice just for the installation by clicking on Add and Save & Close.

5. This brings you back to the Sales Transactions list. Clear the filter so that you can see all the transactions. Note that this table is sorted by date, but you can sort by any column header by clicking on the header. If you don't see the columns you need, click on the Gear icon and choose the columns you want to display.

Step by Step: Receive Payment

1. Next step is to receive payment. Let's say that your customer sent you a check payment of 300$. Click on Receive Payment next to the customer's name.

2. A listing of Outstanding Transactions shows up with the invoice checked. You can deposit to Undeposited Funds or directly into a bank account. If you're signed up for QuickBooks Payments, you could process a credit card here. You'll learn more about payments later in the guide. Choose Undeposited Funds and Save and Close.

3. From the Sales Transactions page, you can enter transactions based on currently listed transaction or can create new sales transactions from the drop down at the top of the page.

4. Entering Transactions from the Quick Create

5. If you have the expanded view of Quick Create opened, you can see a listing of sales type transactions under the Customers column.

Step by Step: Entering Delayed Charge

1. Click on Delayed Charge. A delayed charge is a non-posting transaction and what you're telling QuickBooks is that you need to invoice a customer for something, but don't want to invoice for it now. Let's say you are a landscaping service and you do gardening for multiple customers. Every day you record the where you performed a service that day but you only invoice once a month. You can record that activity in QuickBooks as a Delayed Charge and at month end easily create an invoice.

2. Enter the desired customer's name and in the date field type W to go to the beginning of the week. Enter the desired service under the Product and Service column. Enter 4 under the quantity columns and $35 under the rate column. Click on Save and New

3. Enter the customer's name and in the date field type K and the plus key (+). K brings us to the end of this week and the plus (+) key advances a day which brings us to the beginning of next week. Enter the performed service under the Product and Service column. Enter 3 under the

quantity columns and $35 under the rate column. Click on Save and Close.

Step by Step: Creating an Invoice from Quick Create

1. From Quick Create choose Invoice.

2. Enter the customer's name. As soon as you enter the customer name, if there are any unbilled (delayed) charges or unbilled time, a drawer opens on the right so that you can easily add them to the invoice.

3. Click on Add all and Save and Close.

Step by Step: Recurring Transactions

What happens if you have monthly recurring charges and you don't want to have to remember to enter them? Even better, you'd like QuickBooks to automatically create an invoice and email it to your customers. Use the Recurring Transactions feature. Most transactions (sales, purchases and journal entries) can be made recurring.

1. From Quick Create click Invoice.

2. Type in the desired customer's name and choose the performed service under Product/Service. Leave the quantity at 1 and the rate at $35.00. At the bottom of the screen click on Make recurring.

3. This opens a screen where you can create a recurring invoice template. You can name the template, say whether you want it automatically entered, choose to automatically send an email and, if scheduled, set up the schedule. Save the template.

4. You have a lot of flexibility when creating a template. Experiment with it in the sample file. Note that if you have an already recorded transaction and want to make it recurring, open it up and click on Make recurring at the bottom of the screen. Remember most transactions can be made recurring.

Step by Step: Recurring Transaction List

1. To see a list of recurring transactions, click on the Gear icon and open Recurring Transactions under Lists.

2. From here you can add new templates, edit an existing template, use or delete.

3. Expense and Purchase Transaction

4. Whenever you set up a new area of QuickBooks, you need to review the company settings related to that area. Before you go into the Company Settings, you need to make sure you understand the different types of expense and purchase transactions.

5. Bill – a transaction that you enter when you receive a bill from a vendor but don't want to pay it until later. This is available in Essentials and Plus only Expense – a way to enter cash, check or credit card purchases

6. Checks – a way to enter transactions that reduce your bank account. If the transaction is truly a check, you can print checks

7. Bill Payment – transaction used to pay the bills entered. This is available in Essentials and Plus only

8. Purchase Order – use a purchase order to tell a vendor that you want to order goods or services. This is available in Plus only

9. Vendor Credit – enter a vendor credit to record either a refund or return from a vendor. This is available in Essentials and Plus only

10. Credit Card Credit – this transaction records a credit card refund from a vendor

11. All these transactions relate to monies going out. Some of these transactions can be launched from more than one access point whereas others can be launched only from one.

12. Determine Appropriate Expense-Related Settings

13. Company Settings

14. Click on the Gear icon to access the Company Settings. There are four tabs along the left-hand side to set the preferences as to how you want to use the company file. Expenses has its own category, but there are also expense settings under the Advanced Settings. Bills and expenses preferences allow you to use items, track purchases by the customer and mark them billable. Note, whether you can utilize these preferences depends on your level of subscription. Here's also where you turn on using Purchase Orders. Under the Advanced tab, you have the same types of automation choices that we saw with customers. Do you want QBs to automatically apply bill payments? Think about it before you turn it on. Under the Miscellaneous sections it's a good idea to turn on the duplicate check and bill warnings.

15. Recognize Alternative Entry Points For Entering Purchasing Transactions

Vendor Center

The Vendor Center, accessed by selecting Vendors in the left navigation bar, is a dashboard for adding, editing and reviewing vendors with which your client QuickBooks Online company does business. The list of Vendors can be printed or exported, and it can be sorted by various parameters or filtered. Beside each Vendor listing is an Action column which has a drop-down box from which to create transactions such as bills or checks or to make a vendor inactive. In addition, you can email vendors in batch by using the Batch Actions drop-down list. These emails can use your choice of web-based email or email client.

Step by Step: Creating a Bill

1. In the Action list select on Create bill for the desired customer. Side note: Because of the company setting, you have the choice to post directly to an account on the chart of accounts or use an item off the Products and Services List or combination.

2. Under Account details enter Advertising for $2,500, billable to customer for which you performed the said advertising

3. Use the keyboard shortcut Ctrl + Alt + S to save.

4. Enter a second bill for another desired customer for, let's say, Meals and Entertainment, $250.00 and Save and Close.

5. Notice that when you use your keyboard shortcut, QuickBooks saves the transactions and assumes you wish to enter an additional transaction of the same type. But QuickBooks does not assume you wish to use the same vendor, so, in this case, you needed to enter the second

customer as the vendor. The Vendor Center now shows two open bills for the said customer.

Step by Step: Paying Bills

1. From the Action column, click on Make payment next to the customer's name. QuickBooks opens the Bill Payment screen with the outstanding bills listed and check marked for you to pay. At the top of the screen, you can choose to pay via bank account or credit card.

2. At the bottom of the screen click on Save and close.

3. As with the Customer Center, you can drill down on the vendor name and get a listing of transactions that you can act on or create new transactions from the drop-down list on the right.

4. Entering Transactions -> Expenses

5. As you learned earlier, if you click on Expenses under Transactions on the Navigation bar, QuickBooks opens a listing of the last 365 days of transactions. This screen can be filtered to modify the view. You can drill down on any transaction. You can also enter a new transaction or print checks.

Step by Step: Entering Expense Type of Transaction

1. On the New Transaction drop-down menu choose Expense. To recap what was said earlier, an Expense type

of transaction allows you to either reduce your bank account or increase your credit card payable for a purchase made for the company. This is a good transaction type to use for your "shoebox" clients. They bring in a whole box full of expense receipts that are marked as to whether they used a credit card, check or cash. Rather than having to sort through them and putting them into piles by payment type, you can just enter on this expense screen.

2. Enter an expense for the desired vendor. It was paid with a Mastercard and it was for Dues & Subscriptions for $10.

3. At the bottom of your screen click on Save and New.

4. Enter a transaction for another of your vendors. It was paid out of Checking with manual check #32. It was for Commissions and Fees for $100. Save and Close.

5. On the Expense Transactions page, both expenses show up, but one affected the bank account and the other a credit card account. If you are entering all checks, use the Check feature, rather than the Expense transaction.

Step by Step: Paying Multiple Bills

1. Previously you learned how to pay one bill at a time. You paid the bill from the Vendor Center and it also could be

paid from the Expense Transactions page. If you want to pay multiple bills for multiple vendors at one time, you need to access Pay Bills from Quick Create.

2. Click on Quick Create and choose Pay Bills.

3. Select Checking as the Payment Account.

4. Select which bills to pay, enter the payment date and payment method Printed Check.

5. Note that in the upper right-hand corner you can sort how you want to see the bills listed. Click on Pay Bills.

6. If you click on Pay and Print, QuickBooks will give you a list of bills paid as well as print the checks. Because you chose the payment method of Printed Check but didn't print them now, they can be batch printed, which you'll learn about shortly.

Step by Step: Create a Check (write a check to pay a bill)

1. Click on Quick Create and choose Check.

2. Enter the vendor: for instance, Diego's Road Warrior Bodyshop. If you enter a vendor name and there is an outstanding bill related to that vendor, a drawer pops up on the right-hand side of the page and allows you to add the bill to the check. The accounting effect is to decrease the bank accounts and decrease Accounts Payable. This

feature will help prevent clients from making the mistake of writing a check for a bill already entered and posting it to an expense account.

3. Click Add to add the bill to the check. This changes the transaction type from Check to Bill Payment. Save and Close.

4. If this check really wasn't to pay an outstanding bill, enter the account or item details.

Step by Step: Print Checks in Batch

1. Click on Quick Create and choose Print Checks.

2. Now, you'll want to check if your cheques are lined up. If they are, they'll be susceptible to you marking them for printing.

3. Choose which ones to print and Preview and Print. Before you do that, you'll need to make sure the starting check number is correct.

4. Transactions -> Banking

5. The Banking Center allows you to link your bank and credit card accounts to QuickBooks. Once that is done QuickBooks automatically downloads transactions nightly, though you can download manually by clicking on Update in the upper right-hand corner.

Step by Step: Using the Banking Center

1. Under Transactions on the Navigation bar, click on Banking.

2. At the top of the screen, the linked bank and credit card accounts are displayed as well as the number of transactions that have been downloaded and need to be either entered or matched. Although QuickBooks downloads transactions nightly, you can click on Update to import the latest transaction.

3. If your bank account does not connect to QuickBooks, the drop down on the Update icon allows you to import CSV, QFX, QBO or OFX formatted files. You can also add accounts by clicking on the icon next to the Update icon. Another option under the Update drop-down menu allows you to create and manage rules. You'll do that after you understand the different parts of the Banking Center. In the middle, there are tabs for New Transactions, In QuickBooks and Excluded.

4. New transactions – These are the newly downloaded transactions. They are the ones that you need to act on.

5. In QuickBooks – These are transactions that have been matched or added from the New Transactions tab. Although there are none in the sample file, once you start

using the Banking Center in a live file, you will see many transactions listed there.

6. Excluded – These are downloaded transactions that you have decided not to enter into QuickBooks. Typically, it is because they've already been entered and reconciled. Already reconciled transactions will not show up as a match. This typically occurs when you are first using the Banking Center.

7. A listing of downloaded transactions shows up on the next part of the page. The default is to show All downloaded transactions, but you may see a tab for Recognized transactions. These are transactions that are either matched, or QuickBooks has guessed how you want to enter based on past transactions and rules. You might want to take care of those first just to clean up the list. Notice to the far right there is a Printer icon and a Gear icon. You can print the list of transactions.

8. Click on the Gear icon. You can set preferences as to which columns you want to see and how many rows you want to see in the Banking Center.

9. Click on Copy Description. This feature tells QuickBooks to automatically copy the bank's transaction description to the Memo field. The Memo field can show up on reports. It's also useful for troubleshooting entries. You

can edit the memo before adding to QuickBooks. The transactions can be sorted by any column. As you scroll down, notice that in the category or match list that QuickBooks has already matched several transactions.

10. Click on the column header Category or Match

11. QuickBooks automatically looks for a match. The match could be against a check, bill payment, deposits, payment received from the customer, etc. If upon a quick review, you agree, you can match each one individually by clicking on match in the action list. Alternatively, if you want to enter several transactions at one time select the first transaction you want to enter, hold your shift key down and click on the last transaction you want to enter, click on the down arrow on Batch actions and accept selected. That matches the downloaded transaction against a transaction that was already entered into QuickBooks.

12. Click on the selection box for Hicks Hardware. Hold your shift key down and click on the selection box for Hall Properties. By holding down your Shift key, QuickBooks selects all the transactions between Hicks Hardware and Hall Properties.

13. Click on the Batch Actions drop-down list and choose Accept Selected. Those transactions move from the New Transactions tab to the In QuickBooks tab.

14. Go back to the New Transactions tab and click on the column header for Description. There are two expense transactions for A Rental. QuickBooks does not know the vendor name or the account to use.

15. Type in A Rental in the Payee field. There is no name in QuickBooks for A Rental. Add it on the fly as a vendor.

16. Choose Equipment Rental as the posting account. As soon as you do that, QuickBooks assumes you want the second transaction for A Rental to use the A Rental vendor and post to Equipment Rental. You could add each transaction individually or click on the selection boxes and under Batch Actions, choose Accept Selected as you did earlier in this exercise. If you need to split the transaction you can easily do so by clicking on Split.

17. Locate the vendor in question in the middle of the page. QuickBooks does not know where to post this transaction.

18. Click on the Update drop down and choose Manage Rules

19. Click on New rule.

20. Enter the mentioned vendor as the rule name and in the Description field.

21. Select the said vendor as the Payee and Supplies as the Category.

22. Click on Save.

23. Click on Bank and Credit Cards.

The vendor now shows Supplies as the posting account and indicates that this account was set by a rule. This rule was very simple. You can create some complex rules. For example, if the vendor's is less than $500, post to Supplies. Then create a second rule that states if the same vendor's is greater than $500, post to Equipment. You can also create rules for splits. For example, a vendor's transactions should be split 40% Internet and 60% to Telephone. When you click on a transaction in the Banking Center there are three radio buttons.

You've been working with Add. If you think there should be a match, change the radio button to Find match and QBs will try and find matching transactions. If you can't find it, as mentioned before — it may be because the transaction was already reconciled in QBs. If that's the case, and you don't want to enter that transaction, because it's already in QBs, check the box and under the Batch Actions — say Exclude Selected. The Transfer button is used to indicate that this transaction is a transfer between two company accounts.

Identify Additional Transactions Initiated Using The Quick Create Menu

There are miscellaneous other types of transactions that can be accessed from the Quick Create function. One case in which a transaction can only be accessed via Quick Create function is time tracking. Time can be tracked using the Single Time Activity or the Weekly Timesheet function. This feature can be used even if you are not signed up for QuickBooks Online Payroll.

Step by Step: Fill out a Single Time Activity

1. Select Quick Create (+) at the top of the QuickBooks Online window.

2. If necessary, select Show More.

3. Under Employees select Single Time Activity.

4. Enter the name of the Employee or Vendor whose time is being tracked.

5. Enter the date for which the time is being tracked. 6. Enter the Customer for whom the time is being tracked.

6. Enter the Service being rendered during this time.

7. If Billable preference is turned on, check if the time is billable and the billing rate.

8. Enter the time tracked as, for example, 3.5 hours, either in HH:MM format (3:30) or in decimal format (3.5). Or, check the box next to Enter Start & End Times and then fill in the fields for Start Time and End Time.

9. Enter a description of the work done.

10. Select Save and close or (by clicking on the drop-down box next to Save and Close) select Save and New.

Step by Step: Fill out a Weekly Timesheet

1. Select Quick Create (+) at the top of the QuickBooks Online window.

2. If necessary, select Show More.

3. Under Employees select Weekly Timesheet.

4. Enter the name of the Employee or Vendor whose time is being tracked.

5. Enter the work week for which the time is being tracked (the preferred first day of a work week for this company is determined in the Company Settings for Time Tracking).

6. In each row of the Weekly Timesheet grid, enter the Customer for this individual's time is being tracked, the Service being rendered during this time, and the time tracked day by day during the week, either in HH:MM

format (e.g., 3:30) or in decimal format (e.g., 3.5). If necessary, for invoicing purposes, enter the Bill @ rate and the Taxable status as well.

7. Select Save and close or (by clicking on the drop-down box next to Save and Close) select Save and New.

Step by Step: Make a Bank Deposit

1. Select Quick Create (+) at the top of the QuickBooks Online window.

2. If necessary, select Show More.

3. Under Other select Bank Deposit.

4. Select which bank account you are using for the deposit.

5. Fill in the date.

6. If there are any monies in Undeposited Funds, they will show up on the top part of the screen.

7. Select the Existing Payments if they are part of the deposit.

8. In the Add New Deposits area, add any other payments received, typically non sales related transactions.

9. If you are taking cash back from the deposit, click in the posting account, (i.e., Petty Cash or Owner's Draw), and the amount of cash be taken.

10. Click on Save and Close or Save and New.

11. You can also print a Deposit Slip and Summary using preprinted deposit slips or a Summary Only that you can print on plain paper.

12. You can write a check for any kind of expense that you track with QuickBooks expense accounts and for a non-inventory part, service, and other charge items. If you are using inventory or purchase orders, you can write checks for inventory part items too.

13. To write a check:

14. Go to the Banking menu and click Write Checks.

15. Click the Bank Account drop-down arrow and then click the account from which you want to write the check. If the vendor has not already been set-up in QuickBooks, it will ask of you to add the new vendor. If the vendor was previously added to the vendors list and address information was provided, QuickBooks will automatically fill in the address for that vendor on the check.

16. Fill in the on-screen check as you would a paper check.

17. Itemize your expenses (shipping charges, taxes, or other expenses not associated with any one item) on the Expenses tab.

18. If you are purchasing items for your inventory, enter the items on the Items tab.

19. When you are finished entering all the pertinent information, click "Save & Close" or "Save & New" if you have more checks to write. Also, you may use the "Previous" and "Next" navigation buttons in the top-left to view checks that have been written

20. To find and print a single check:

21. Load the blank check form into the printer.

22. Go to the Banking menu and click Write Checks.

23. Click the Find button and search for the check you want to print.

24. Double-click to view the check you want to print.

25. Click Print.

26. In the Print Checks window, choose the options you want and click Print.

Entering Bills

At first glance, entering bills in QuickBooks and then paying them later might seem like more work than just writing checks. But as you'll learn in this chapter, there are several advantages to entering bills in QuickBooks, and the program makes it incredibly easy to pay them

You are advised to enter bills immediately upon receiving them and paying them afterwards. Use the Enter Bills window for entering of bills upon receival. Then use the Pay Bills window for payment of the bills. You can set up QuickBooks to remind you to pay bills when they are due to be paid. Using this method, you keep your money in your business for as long as possible. You might still use a check to pay the bill, but this method enables you to track quantity of the money you owe. And at any time, you can run reports to analyze unpaid bills for information such as to which vendors you owe money. Do not simply write a check in the Write Checks window to pay bills that you entered in the accounts payable register or the Enter Bills window. Use the Pay Bills window to pay these bills.

- Click on the "Enter Bills" icon on your homepage. The "Enter Bills" window will open to record your bill.

- Enter the pertinent information, including vendor, date, amount due, and the bill due date into the Bill template. (If the vendor is not already set-up in QuickBooks, you will be prompted to set it up here).

- As with writing checks, the two tabs below the Bill template allow you to associate the bill with specific expense accounts or specify specific items. You can select the account or item by using the drop-down box that will appear or by typing in the expense account or item and enter information the same as when writing checks.

- If the bill is associated with an account or items that are not yet created in QuickBooks, you can create them by selecting "Add New" and adding the account or item.

- When you are finished entering all the pertinent information, click "Save & Close" or "Save & New" if you have more bills to enter.

- Make sure your preferences are set to remind you of due bills if you would like to be reminded. Select Edit → Preferences from the toolbar. Choose "Reminders" from the left-hand preferences list and select the "Company Preferences" tab. Here you can change the reminder settings, including the time frame for the reminders.

Paying Bills

Entering bills in QuickBooks isn't the same as paying bills. The bills you enter in your company file are a record of what you owe and when, but they do nothing to send money to your vendors. Pay Bills is the QuickBooks feature that pushes your money out the door. It lets you select the bills you want to pay, how much to pay on each one, as well as the payment method, account, and date. If you have credits or early payment discounts, you can include those, too.

- Click on the "Pay Bills" icon on your homepage. The "Pay Bills" window will open, showing you a list of all your entered bills.

- Select the bill or bills you wish to pay, the payment date, the method of payment, and the account you are using to pay the bill(s). If you pay with a check, you can opt to print checks in QuickBooks or indicate the check number of your written check. QuickBooks will decrease the amount in your checking account by the amount of 17 the paid bills. If you paid with a credit card, QuickBooks will increase the amount you owe on your credit card account in accordance with the paid bills.

- Click "Pay Selected Bills" and QuickBooks will automatically write a check (if you selected check as your method of payment) and adjust the associated accounts to reflect the bill payment.

- You are not required to go through Pay Bills window to be able to pay them. You can enter checks, credit card payments, and cash expenditures directly in the appropriate registry. Though, if you enter bills via the enter bills window, or the accounts payable register, you are required to use the pay bills window for your bill payment. Do not use the Write Checks window to pay a bill that you have entered with either of these methods.

At any time, you can go to the vendor center and see all your vendors and those with whom you have balances listed at the left-hand side of the vendor center. Above the vendors list, you can select to view all vendors or just those with whom you have open balances by selecting from the drop-down box under "Vendors." In the lower portion of the vendor center, you can see a list of all your transactions with vendors including bills, bill payments, checks, etc. You can also select specific types of transactions and specific time periods using the drop-down boxes above the transactions list.

CHAPTER 4

Banking Transactions Managing

By synchronizing your real-world bank accounts with the bank accounts in QuickBooks, you can download your bank balances and transactions into your QuickBooks company file, so you'll always be able to know the state of your wallet. (The connection you set up between the two is called bank feeds in QuickBooks, to differentiate it from online banking that you perform by logging into your bank account outside of QuickBooks.) That way, before repaying your aunt the start-up money she lent you, you can quickly update your QuickBooks accounts, check your balance, and be certain that you aren't giving her a check that bounces.

Besides managing your cash flow, banking online is much more convenient than the old paper-based methods of yesteryear. For example, you already have a lot of transactions in your QuickBooks account register (from receiving payments against invoices or making payments to your vendors) and you can easily match these transactions to the ones you download from the bank so you know how much money you really have in your account—and whether someone is helping themselves to your money without permission. Plus, you can transfer money between your money market account and your checking account when you find yourself awake at 2 a.m.

Banking online also lets you pay bills without having to write checks, lick stamps, or walk to the mailbox. After you submit payment transactions online, the billing service you use either transfers funds from your bank account to the vendors or generates and mails paper checks. Online billing also lets you set up recurring bills so you can go about your business without worrying about missing a payment. All this convenience requires some setup. QuickBooks needs to know how to connect to your bank, and your bank needs to know that you want to use its online services. This chapter explains how to apply for online services with your financial institution and set up bank feeds in QuickBooks to perform all these tasks. Once your accounts and bank feeds are set up and online services activated, you'll learn what you need to know about taking transactions through the internet, as well as online payments. And if you enter transactions in your company file, you'll also learn about matching them with the ones you download—and correcting any discrepancies.

Banking Accounts Linking

QuickBooks can zip you through the two basic ways of producing and distributing invoices and other forms: on paper and electronically. Within those two camps, you can choose to produce and send forms as soon as you complete them or place them in a queue to process in batches. For sporadic forms, it's easier to print or email them as you go. But when you generate dozens or even hundreds of sales orders, invoices, statements, or checks, printing and emailing batches is a much better use of your time. If you have workhorse transactions that you enter again and again, QuickBooks can memorize them and then fill in most, if not all, of the fields in future transactions for you. For transactions that happen on a regular schedule—like monthly customer invoices or vendor bills—the program can remind you when it's time to record the transaction, or even add the transaction without any help from you. You can also memorize transactions that you use occasionally, such as estimates, and call on them only when you need them. QuickBooks' search features can help you track down financial info, which you can appreciate if you've ever hunted frantically for a transaction. Whether you want to correct a billing problem on a customer's invoice, check whether you paid a vendor's bill, or look for the item you want to add to an estimate, QuickBooks gives you several ways to search. You can look for different types of transactions within various date ranges in the Customer, Vendor, and Employee Centers—and the Inventory Center, if you use QuickBooks Premier or Enterprise. The Item List window sports a few search boxes for finding the items you want. Form windows, such as Create Invoices, have a Find button on their Main tabs so you can quickly find transactions of the corresponding type. You can use the program's Search feature to search throughout your company file or QuickBooks. And the full-blown Find feature is perfect for surgical searches.

On the Dashboard, under Bank Accounts, click Connect account. First, find your bank. Then fill in the username and password you use to access your accounts. Click Sign In when you're finished. Once connected, you'll see all the accounts you have at this bank. Choose the account you use for your business and tell QuickBooks what kind of account it is. QuickBooks will download all the transactions from the last 90 days—but these transactions aren't in QuickBooks yet. The first time QuickBooks downloads your transactions it's up to you to review and categorize your expenses. On the Banking page, click on the Category or Match column to sort the transactions. You'll see where QuickBooks tried to find categories for some transactions. Click the first transaction in the list to open it. To give this transaction a different category, open the transaction menu and choose the right one. Then click Add to save the transaction. You can get a summary of how your business is doing right on your dashboard. You can also run reports like the Profit and Loss report which will give you more detail about how your expenses are categorized and where you're spending the majority of your business' money.

Importing, Matching and Adding of Transactions

Among the myriad of benefits provided by QuickBooks Online is that it can save you a lot of time you would unnecessary waste by manual input of each bank transaction by simply downloading all of them automatically. Nearly every big bank will let you to easily and quickly connect to QB, though, it should be noted that several smaller banks and unions simply do not have that option. In order to import transactions into QB, your online banking ID and password are required to log in. However, this is only asked of you the first time, as QB stays connected to your bank account for the purpose of downloading day-to-day transactions.

- In the Left Menu Bar, select Banking. To locate your bank/financial institution, you can do one of the following: enter the name of your bank in the search field or click on the bank list below and find it manually. Punch in the ID and password you would normally enter to access your bank account. Your bank shows every account you have with them. Be sure to select only the business accounts that you want to connect to QuickBooks.

- Select every account you wish to be connected to QB by simply clicking anywhere in the account row

- Account Name: From the drop list, click the QB account that you wish to connect with the bank account. In case you still haven't set up the bank account in QB, click Add on the account drop list.

- The account setup window will pop up. Fill in the blanks in order to set up the bank account in QB

- Account Type: Choose the type of account for which you want to import transactions into QuickBooks. Normally, this is either a bank account or a credit card one.

- Detail Type: Here you wish to provide more info on the category of the bank account.

- Name: How will the account name be displayed in QuickBooks.

- Description: Enter the name of the bank and the type of the account (e.g., checking, savings, etc.)

- Save and Close: Double-check to make sure that you have made selections in all five fields. Click the Save and Close button.

Bank Deposits Recording

The Make Deposits window is like an electronic deposit slip. The payments you chose to deposit are already filled in. If you have other checks to deposit besides customer payments, they don't automatically show up in this window, however, if you're keen on adding them, you can do so manually. If you're depositing a payment made in a foreign currency, in the "Exchange Rate 1 [currency] =" box, type the exchange rate that your bank used for the transaction. The table of deposits then shows the deposit amount in the foreign currency, and the lower section of the window shows the deposit total in both the foreign currency and your home currency. After you make your foreign-currency deposits, you can see how much you gained or lost due to changes in the exchange rate by choosing Reports→Company & Financial→Realized Gains & Losses. This report shows the payment amounts in your home currency, the exchange rate, and the resulting gain or loss.

You need to record a deposit in QuickBooks if you receive a check from someone other than a customer. To begin, in the Homepage, select the Plus sign in the top and select Bank Deposit right below the Other column on the far right. The record deposit window will display the following:

- Bank account – Choose from the drop list that one account that you want to deposit this check to.

- Balance – this is the current balance of the bank account you selected.

- Date –the date you will make the deposit

- Received From – select from the drop down the person or business that you received the check from. If they weren't set up in QB, you can do so here by selecting Add new from the drop-down menu.

- Account – select from the drop down the account that you want to track this deposit.

- Description – type a description here that will help you to identify what this check was for.

- Payment method – select the payment method.

- Ref no. – if the payment method is a check, type the check number in this field. Otherwise, you can leave this field blank.

- Amount – enter the amount of the deposit.

- Cashback goes to: select the petty cash account here if you plan to get cash back.

- Cashback memo: indicate here if there is a specific purpose for the cash back

- Cashback amount: enter the amount of cashback you plan to receive from this deposit.

- This is the total amount of the deposit less the cash back amount.

Once you have completed all the fields, Save and Close. When you're moving money between bank accounts, if you simply accept the Online Banking transactions (see next section), you may accidentally create two unrelated transactions. We want to transfer $500 from the Checking account to the Savings account. Select + | Transfer. Enter the accounts to transfer the money to and from, the amount of the transfer, and the date of the transfer.

It would be helpful to put a description of the transaction in the memo field. If this transfer happens on a regular basis, then you can make it a recurring transaction. Click Make Recurring to set this up. Click Save. You can save several hours a week of clerical tasking by using Online Banking. It is found under Transactions | Banking. This feature works in one of two ways:

- A direct connection to your bank or credit card company. It "sucks in" all that day's transactions for your approval. Some banks charge for this service.

- Download the month's transactions from your bank's website and import them into QuickBooks Online.

This service is always free but may be labor-intensive. If you do have Direct Connect, you can finish each day, as part of the '15-Minute Books', by opening Online Banking. Any transactions that you entered manually into your QB will be marked as "Matched."

For transactions that don't match, click on them to edit. If it's a Vendor who you will use frequently, update the Payee line. If it's a one-off expense or a Payee you don't want to accumulate in your Vendor list (like a restaurant or a gas station), leave this field blank or create a generic Payee (like "Restaurant" or "Gas Station"). Next, modify the Expense category. Be sure to choose the right one and be very sure not to leave it as Uncategorized Income or Uncategorized Expense! When done, select Accept. For Deposits, this is usually when I go to + | Bank Deposit to gather the corresponding individual transactions. As soon as we're done, QBO notices the new matching dollar amount and Matches the transaction. Every time you label a new type of transaction, QBO will create a Rule, so the next time it sees that same Payee from the bank, it will modify this entry automatically.

Sometimes one Payee might have two different types of transactions. For example, Intuit is my Payee for the Dues and Subscriptions for my QBO account. Intuit is also the vendor for my Merchant Services Fees account, and I have to keep an eye on each transaction to be sure it gets filed appropriately. In another scenario, some banks only provide generic Memos like "Check", and Online Banking will autofill it with the most recent previous transaction. Fortunately, you can create manual Rules to control these situations. If the transaction is a Transfer between bank accounts, also make sure it's marked as a Transfer using the radio buttons above the Payee. Otherwise, you'll wind up with two transactions indicating money in and money out instead. While it still needs maintenance to import cleanly, this new feature automates the time-consuming task of manually entering every single debit card and credit card charge. It also helps you discover transactions you missed, or ones you created that never hit the bank.

CHAPTER 5

Business Credit Card Transaction Managing

In QuickBooks, the credit cards you use can be set up as accounts or vendors, depending on how you prefer to record your credit card transactions. Here's the deal: tracking credit card charges using an account has several advantages. With a credit card account in QB, charges can be entered as they happen (which takes no time at all if you download credit card transactions;). Then, when you receive your statement, you can reconcile the credit card account as you would a checking account, so you can see whether your records and your charge card company's match. To prevent credit card charge payee names from filling your Vendor List with entries you don't need, store names in the Memo cell or create more general vendors like Gas, Restaurant, and Office Supplies.

Credit card vendor.

If you set up a credit card as a vendor, you don't have an account to reconcile when you receive your credit card statement. In addition, the name of every establishment you bless with credit card purchases won't fill up your Vendor List. The drawback to this approach is that you still must allocate the money you spent to the appropriate accounts, and you can't download that split transaction from your credit card company. With statement in hand, open the Enter Credit Card Charges window (choose Banking→Enter Credit Card Charges) to enter a single transaction allocating the total statement balance to each of the charges you made. (On the window's Expenses and Items tabs, add entries to allocate charges to the appropriate expense accounts.) That way, the transaction does double-duty by reconciling your charges to the statement, which will make your accountant happy

When you import transactions from your business credit cards into QuickBooks, they are un-posted. This simply means that you need to review them and provide some additional information before they can be added to your register in QuickBooks. Here we will show you how to review and categorize your credit card transactions so that they can be added to your register and financial statements.

At the top of the Banking Center, all the bank and credit card accounts that you have set up are at the very top of the page.

If the account is linked to your bank account, the top blue portion of the account box will show the credit card balance as of the date of the last sync.

- The bottom portion of the account box displays the current balance in the QuickBooks register and the number of transactions in the For Review tab below.

- If the account is not linked, it will show $0.00 in the top portion of the box.

- Similar to the linked account, the bottom portion of the account box displays the current balance in the QuickBooks register and the number of transactions in the For Review tab.

Business Credit Card Transaction Managing

- Bank feed transactions are organized into the following three tabs:

- For Review – this tab will show all the un-posted transactions. For example, when you import transactions into QuickBooks, this is where they will appear until you review them and act.

- In QuickBooks – this tab will show all the transactions that have been matched or added to the register in QuickBooks.

- Excluded – this tab will show transactions removed from the For-Review tab by you.

- To manage downloaded credit card transaction in the bank center, from the home page, click on Transactions located on the left-hand menu bar and select Banking. You should begin with the transactions that are in the "for review" tab. Within this tab, transactions are categorized into two additional tabs:

- All – this tab will list all transactions (including those on the Recognized tab)

- Recognized – If QuickBooks recognizes a transaction that is already recorded in your register, it will display a green MATCH tag next to the transaction and add it to the Recognized tab as indicated below.

- To add the transaction to the register, just click the Match link located in the Action column indicated below. QuickBooks will add the transaction to the QuickBooks register and include it in your financial statements.

Most people tend to be creatures of habit. Whether you are running out to grab lunch or to the office supply store to get ink for the printer, you will most likely purchase these items from the same retailers. QuickBooks will recognize vendor names or descriptions that you have previously downloaded and will make suggestions as to which account transactions should be coded to. If you accept the suggested account, QuickBooks will change the account for all transactions of that same name.

For example, if you have previously coded Bluehost.com transactions to your Advertising account, then the next time a Bluehost.com transaction is downloaded, QuickBooks will suggest coding it to the Advertising account. If you accept the suggestion, then QuickBooks will categorize all transactions with the Bluehost.com description to the Advertising account.

If a customer returns a product or finds an overcharge on her last invoice, you have two choices: Issue a credit against her balance or issue a refund by writing her a check. In the bookkeeping world, the documents that explain the details of a credit are called credit memos. On the other hand, when a customer doesn't want to wait to get the money she's due or isn't planning to purchase anything else from you, a refund check is the logical solution. In either case, refunds and credits both begin with a credit memo.

When you purchase items using your business credit card, you may need to return something because it was damaged, or it just didn't work out. The vendor will usually process the return using the same credit card that you used to make the purchase. When this credit shows up on your credit card statement, you need to be sure that it is flagged as a credit card refund and that it is coded to the same account you coded the original purchase to.

From the Home page, click on the Gear icon to the left of the company name and select Chart of Accounts. From the chart of accounts list, click on the View Register link next to the credit card as indicated below. The Credit Card register will display. From the drop-down, select CC Credit. Complete the following fields:

- Account – From the drop-down, be sure that you are in the correct register. If not, select the credit card that you need to enter the credit return for. This is the credit card that the vendor credited the purchase to.

- Date – Enter the date that you returned the product.

- Ref No./Type is a field you don't have to fill out. It is recommended that you put CREDIT. Below the ref no. field is the transaction type. QuickBooks will put the transaction type based on your prior selection.

- Payee – From the drop-down, select the vendor that you returned the product to.

- Memo – Include any additional information about the return in this field (e.g. reason for return).

- Payment – Enter the cost of the item that was returned.

- Account – From the drop-down, select the account that the credit for the return should be categorized to. It is best practice to use the same account that you categorized the original purchase for the credit card refund.

- Save – After you complete all the fields, you can save this transaction.

If you need to edit a credit card refund that was previously entered, you can do so by following these steps:

- From the Home page, click on the Gear icon to the left of company name, and select Chart of Accounts.

- From the drop-down, select the credit card that you entered the refund for.

- Click anywhere within the transaction to activate the fields that you can make changes to.

- Once you have made your changes, be sure to save them

Business Credit Card Reconciling

You've opened your mail, plucked out the customer payments, and deposited them in your bank account. In addition to that, you've paid your bills. Now you can sit back and relax knowing that most of the transactions in your bank and credit card accounts are accounted for. What's left? Some stray transactions might pop up—an insurance claim check to deposit or handling the aftermath and bank fees for a customer's bounced check, to name a few. Plus, running a business typically means that money moves between accounts—from interest-bearing accounts to checking accounts, from PayPal to your checking account, or from merchant credit card accounts to savings.

For any financial transaction you perform, QuickBooks has a way to enter it, whether you prefer the guidance of transaction windows or the speed of an account-register window. Reconciling your accounts to your bank statements is another key process you don't want to skip. You and your bank can both make mistakes, and reconciling your accounts is the way to catch these discrepancies. Once the bane of bookkeepers everywhere, reconciling is practically automatic now that you can let QuickBooks handle the math. In this chapter, the section on reconciling is the only must-read. And if you want to learn the fastest way to enter any type of bank account transaction, don't skip the first section. You can read about transferring funds, loans, bounced checks, and other financial arcana covered in this chapter as the need arises.

Like your personal credit card accounts, it is important that you reconcile your business credit card accounts on a monthly basis. Reconciling is the process of matching the transactions on your credit card statement to what you have recorded in QuickBooks.

Preparing Business Credit Card reconciliations on a regular basis will help to ensure the following:

- Any discrepancies between your records and the credit card companies are resolved in a timely manner (e.g. a credit card charge that comes through for a different amount from what you authorized.)

- Timely notification of any fraudulent transactions. For example, if you notice transactions listed on your credit card statement that you did not authorize, you can notify the bank as soon as possible so that they can investigate.

In addition, reconciling your credit card transactions in QuickBooks helps ensure every transaction is noted in your books. This helps keep your financial statements, like profit & loss and balance sheet up-to-date.

Before you follow the steps to reconcile, be sure that you have your credit card statement handy for the credit card. We will refer to the credit card statement often during this process.

Here are the steps to reconcile a business credit card account in Quickbooks Online

From the Home page, click on the Gear icon to the left of your company name. Below the Tools column, select Reconcile. Complete the fields as indicated below:

- Account: Select the credit card account you would like to reconcile from the drop down.

- Beginning balance: QB automatically fills in this field with ending balance from the previous month. Check if this amount matches what your bank statement says. If it does not, you should see a notification that says" Hold on! Your account isn't ready to reconcile yet". Click on the "We can help you fix it" link and follow the instructions to resolve the difference before you reconcile the current month.

- Ending balance: Enter the ending balance that appears on your bank-given statement in this field.

- Ending date: Enter the ending date of your bank-given statement in this field.

- Start reconciling: When you are ready, click the "Start reconciling" button to go to the next step.

You will see the following information:

- Statement Ending Balance – The amount that you entered previously in Step 2 will appear in this field. Be sure to doublecheck this because it will cause you to be out of balance if it is incorrect.

- Beginning Balance – As discussed previously, this is the ending balance from last month's statement. QuickBooks will populate this field for you.

- Cleared Balance – As you start to reconcile each item, this amount will change depending on whether you have selected a charge or a payment transaction.

- Charges – This amount will increase as you select charges to reconcile from the detailed section below.

- Payments – This amount will increase as you select payments to reconcile from the detailed section below.

- Difference – Quickbooks will handle this for you. It is the difference between your statement balance and the cleared balance. The goal is to get to a difference of zero.

- Transactions – In this section, you will see all the charges and payments that have been recorded in QuickBooks as of your statement ending date. You can filter this section to just show Charges, Payments or all by clicking on each of the tabs.

If you are new to reconciling, I recommend that you reconcile the area with the least number of transactions first. Our goal is to make sure that every charge and payment listed on the credit card statement is marked as "cleared" in the reconciliation window.

To mark an item as "cleared", click the radio button to the right of the Payments column. Let's start with payments first. Once you have marked all the payments in this window which show in the statement of the credit card, verify that the total payments cleared matches the total payments amount in the statement of the credit card. If the total payments in the statement match the total payments we have "cleared" in QuickBooks, you can move onto charges. However, if your payments do not match, head over to the section for troubleshooting tips on how to fix the out of balance.

Once all charges and payments match the credit card statement, you should have a difference of $0.00. Behind the scenes, QuickBooks will mark all the charges and payments that have been reconciled as cleared. Click the "Finish now" button to generate the credit card reconciliation report. It's important that you save all credit card reconciliation reports for every credit card account. You can create a folder for each credit card account to keep these reports in.

Try some of these tips if you're having trouble getting a $0.00 difference between what's in QuickBooks and what's on your credit card statements:

- If possible, narrow the search down to the transaction type. Figure out whether you aren't in balance with the charges and payments.

- If out of balance for both charges and payments, then tackle them separately. In other words, balance charges/cash advances first and then move onto payments/credits or vice versa.

- Look for the exact dollar amount that you are off. For example, if your difference is $50.00, then look for a transaction for this amount on your credit card statement and then on both the charges section and payments section of the reconcile window.

- Triple check the information that you entered from the credit card statement in step 2 above.

- Check to see if there are any transactions in the reconcile window that you did not select. If the transaction is on your credit card statement, then make sure the radio button next to it is selected.

- If you do have a transaction on the credit card statement that is not in QuickBooks, then you will need to add it to QuickBooks.

CHAPTER 6

Reporting

As if your typical workday isn't hectic enough, the final days of the year bring with them an assortment of additional bookkeeping and accounting tasks. If you've kept on top of your bookkeeping during the year, you can delegate most of these year-end tasks to QuickBooks with just a few clicks. (If you shrugged off your data entry during the year, even the mighty QuickBooks can't help.)

This chapter describes the tasks you have to perform at the end of each fiscal year (or other fiscal period, for that matter) and how to delegate them to QuickBooks. Checking for Problems If you work with an accountant, you may never run a report from the Reports→Accountant & Taxes submenu unless your accountant asks you to. But if you prepare your own tax returns, running the following reports at the end of each year will help sniff out any problems: the Audit Trail report (Reports→Accountant & Taxes→Audit Trail) is especially important if several people work on your company file and transactions seem to disappear or change. QuickBooks' audit trail feature is always turned on, keeping track of changes to transactions, who makes them, and when. You can then check this permanent record by running the Audit Trail report to watch for things like deleted invoices or modifications to transactions after they've been reconciled. (You have to be the QuickBooks administrator or have permission to generate sensitive financial reports to run this report.)

Profit and Loss/Balance Sheet

Reports are critical for feedback and specialized business activities. Their objective is to produce info on the financial standing, as well as conduct and development in the financial position of a company. Reports are expected to be easily understood, important, dependable and analogous. They show assets, liabilities, equity, income and expenses that are precisely linked to a company's financial status. The purpose of reports can impact an owner's critical field choices that might determine further actions in the business. They can be helpful to the management in the way of further clarifying the figures. Also, they may be of use to the management for the annual reports to the shareholders. When you want to find information, the best place to start is a report. From basic financial reports to reports for specialized business activities, being familiar with what's available allows you to quickly locate the information you are looking for. You can use the link on the left navigation bar to access the report center. From here you can easily access report groups, including your customized reports.

It's easy to customize QuickBooks Online reports, so you can quickly develop report formats tailored to your unique business. Once you customize a report, you can have QuickBooks Online save the changes it so that you can run it any time you wish without reconfiguring it. First, we choose a base report that is most like the report we are trying to create. Use the Customize button to access the changes that can be made.

The QuickZoom feature in every report shows the detail behind the reports and lets you drill down to the transaction level. You can display the original transactions and analyze the numbers behind the numbers. From any report, simply hover over the transaction that you would like to open. When the transaction turns blue like a hyperlink, click the transaction. This opens the transaction in a new window so that you can analyze, modify, or notate.

In order to run and read reports effectively, we must understand the fundamentals of reporting. The first thing to know is Cash vs. Accrual. Cash basis reports display income at the time it was received and expenses at the time that they were paid. Accrual basis reports display income at the time it was invoiced and expenses at the time they were incurred. It is key to understand the differences between these reporting methods and the effect that changing the basis can have on your reports. It is good to view accrual-based reports to see income earned and expenses incurred, but it can also be beneficial to view cash-based reports to gain perspective on cash flow. We are now ready to dive into the reports in QuickBooks Online. First, we'll introduce the Report Center, then discuss the Report Groupings and then we'll dive into each group to get to know some of the reports themselves. The Report Center, or Report Dashboard, is where we can find our report categories. Inside each of the categories, we have report groupings to give us reports by topic at the click of a mouse. From the left navigation menu, click Reports. This brings you to the Report Dashboard (or Report Center) where you can access multiple types of reports.

The Report Dashboard first shows a graphical summary of the Profit & Loss, comprised of Income and Expenses. You have an accessible box that allows you to Search reports instead of clicking through the report groups. Then it breaks the reports into four tabs:

- Recommended – The most common reports business owners use is here in the Recommended Reports section. They include Profit & Loss, Balance Sheet, Company

Snapshot, A/R Aging Summary, Expenses by Vendor Summary, A/P Aging Summary. Each of these reports is in their respective report groups as well, but it is faster to access them from here.

- Frequently Run – This section will remember those reports that you run the most often. It will allow you to quickly access regular reports and will change over time depending on what you have frequently run in the recent past.

- My Custom Reports – This is the list of reports you have specifically asked QuickBooks to Save Customizations for. You can run the reports, distribute them, or edit their settings here in this section.

- All Reports – This is where you can access every preset report inside of QuickBooks. The reports are grouped into nine categories based on the purpose of the report. As we dive into the different reports available in QuickBooks Online Plus, we will be exploring ways to customize reports to give us more specific data.

Business Overview reports show different perspectives on how your business is doing. Included in this group are your major financial reports:

Balance Sheet, Profit & Loss, and Statement of Cash Flows with supporting reports Balance Sheet Summary and Profit & Loss

Detail. Also, in this group is your Company Snapshot and Scorecard, which provide graphical representations of your performance inside your company and comparison with the industry. Finally, you can access the Activity Log to see all that has happened in your company file.

First, let's look more in-depth at the financial reports. What are they? Simply, they are reports indicating a company's health. Reading a report is fairly easy. If you can read what ingredients are in a package of soup or baseball stats from last night's baseball game from the morning paper, you can learn to read basic financial reports. The three main financial statements are as follows:

- Balance Sheet – Displays everything a company possesses and what it incurs at a single point in time

- Profit & Loss statement – Displays all the money a company has accumulated and expended in a certain timeframe

- Cash flow statement – Displays the transfer of capital between a company and the outside world in a certain timeframe.

Balance Sheet a.k.a. "What is my business worth?" This report provides a financial snapshot of your company. It is the cover of a book. It lists the balances for each asset, liability, and equity account as of a specific date. It also calculates what your business is worth (the equity) by subtracting what your company owes (liabilities) from everything it owns (assets).

Asset is anything a company possesses that has value. This usually implies they can be sold or used by the company to create product or provide services that can again be sold for profit. Assets include but are not limited to physical property, things that cannot be touched, but still have a value, such as patents or trademark, investments, and of course, cash.

Any amount of money one company owes to another is considered a liability. All kinds of obligations can be viewed as liabilities, such as bank loans, rents, mortgages, payrolls, taxes, environmental cleanup costs, etc. Furthermore, liabilities also encompass obligations to provision of services and/or goods to customers in the future.

Equity is the summary of the net worth of the business (Assets minus Liabilities) as well as the company's interaction with the owners. Are the owners putting money into the business or taking it out or did a new owner invest in the company? These transactions would be summarized in the Equity section.

Step by Step: The Balance Sheet

- Reports -> Recommended Reports -> Balance Sheet

- Notice the list of assets and below them, the list of liabilities

- Click Customize -> Add Sub columns for Comparison -> Select Previous Period

- Run Report.

Profit & Loss, a.k.a "How much money did I make and spend?" This report is also called an income statement. It tells a synopsis of the story. It summarizes your income and expenses for every account you have on your balance sheet, so you can tell if you're operating at a profit or a loss. What shouldn't be forgotten about income is that it is a representation of a time period, as opposed to a balance sheet, which represents a single point in time.

To understand how Profit & Loss reports are constructed, think of them as a flight of stairs. You begin at the top with the full amount of sales and income generated in the accounting period. As you descend down these proverbial stairs, you constantly deduct every expense. When you reach the final stair, after deducting every one of the expenses, you are left with how much the company grossed or lost during the accounting period. This is often called the "the bottom line."

Imagine a new business owner who has designed a new product. He needs to set a few milestones over the next while and here are his goals:

Goal #1: Make sales – The product he designed should be something that will be of value to someone else so that he can receive income, right? That is the first section of profit & loss — Income/Revenues.

Goal #2: Sell the product at a price that will pay for the cost to produce it – If it costs him $5 to create the product each time, then hopefully he is selling it for more than that. The next paragraphs cover the profit & loss – the price of sold goods. This brings us to a Gross Profit amount, which is subtracting the sold goods price from the Total Income.

Goal #3: Sell enough of the product (earn enough income) to cover the costs of running a business (overhead) – It costs money to have a business. The expenses he will have to pay for regardless of selling 1 or 1,000 products are considered overhead. This could be Professional fees, Payroll, Office Rent, Bank Service Charges, and many more. Net Operating Income shows whether this has been accomplished. Goal #4: Earn a profit so you can take some money home – Other things happen like a theft or interest income that are not part of the company's operations. The overall Net Income of the business shows whether this business owner has made any money after everything. Then the owner decides whether to take some home or reinvest it in the company's future.

Step by Step: Profit & Loss

- Reports -> All Reports -> Business Overview->Profit & Loss.

- Notice the list income and below, the list of expenses.

- Click Customize -> Change the Transaction Date to be Last Quarter.

- Change the Accounting Method to be Cash Basis.

- Run Report.

- Company Snapshot

The Company Snapshot report provides an overview of the money coming in and going out of your business, along with the ability to compare your business to others in your industry. To access the report:

- Reports -> All Reports -> Business Overview -> Company Snapshot.

- If prompted, install the Adobe Flash Player plug-in (this will require you to close all browser windows) and then try to access the report again.

- When the report opens you will see the following:

- My Income – In the top-left box, you will see a graphical representation of the five Income accounts with the most income for the selected period. All other accounts are lumped into a category called Other

- My Expenses – The top-right box will show a pie graph of the five Expense accounts with the greatest expenses for the selected period. All other expenses are listed under the Other category

- Previous Year Income and Expense Comparison charts – These charts have been added to allow you to compare income and/or expenses from year to year. You can scroll over the chart itself to see detailed data used to make up the chart you see in this section.

Reporting

- Who Owes Me – the bottom-left box lists all the customers who owe you money and their current open balance amount.

- Whom I Owe – the bottom-right box shows all the vendors you owe money to and your current open balance with them.

- Step by Step: Company Snapshot

- Reports -> All Reports -> Business Overview -> Company Snapshot

- Previous Year Expense Comparison -> Change the Quarterly to Monthly

- Change the All Accounts to Utilities

- See a monthly comparison of the Utilities account last year versus this year

- Scroll over one month to see the exact total.

- Scorecard

Intuit aggregates company data from thousands of small businesses who are using Intuit financial software. The data aggregation is done to be consistent with industry best practices and in alignment with our privacy policy. The aggregated data excludes any company-specific data such as address and telephone number so that any single company cannot be identified individually or by inference. You can compare your performance with those in your industry. Set your Peer Group to be compared to and see how your Net Profit Margin, Sales Growth, and Cash Flow compare to others. Look at the bottom for My Overall Score. The Income and Expense tabs compare over time and details for the date range set and the respective tab you're on to see trends in applicable categories.

Manage Accounts Receivable

Manage Accounts Receivable reports allow you to manage who owes you, and exactly how much they owe you in the hopes of getting paid. The reports include: Customer Balance Summary and Detail, A/R Aging Summary and Detail, Collections Report, Invoice List and Statement List. As a business owner, collecting on money that customers owe the business is one of the least favorite tasks. Use these reports to easily see what is happening and to have direction on which ones to pursue.

Customer Balance Detail a.k.a. "What's the detail behind what customers owe?" The customer balance report lists the customers who owe your company money and how long ago since their invoice for payment. The report displays the unpaid customer balances, grouped by customer and job. It can be very important information for you as a business owner to have, but it is useful to others as well. For example, your company's bank may want to review your customer balance report if you are looking for a loan.

- Step by Step: Customer Balance Detail

- Reports -> All Reports -> Manage Accounts Receivable -> Customer Balance Detail Report

- Notice the columns showing Customers, Dates, Amounts, and Balances.

- Collections Report a.k.a "How do I collect overdue payments?"

- This report lists overdue invoices and unapplied credit memos grouped by customer. It includes when the invoice was due, by how much is the deadline overextended, as well as the customer's phone number. This report is set up almost identical to the Customer Balance Detail report because of the usability. If you are questioning the balance, you have all the details you need and can quickly click into the specific transaction if you need line item detail as well.

- Step by Step: Collections Report

- Reports -> All Reports -> Manage Accounts Receivable -> Collections Report

- Notice the columns showing Customers, Dates, Past Due Amounts and Balances.

- A/R Aging Summary a.k.a. "How long have I been working on collecting money from each customer?"

- The A/R Aging Summary lists each customer with an open balance and lists the open invoices in different columns based on whether it's current or how long it's been overdue (30, 60, and 90+ days).

- Step by Step: A/R Aging Summary

- Reports -> All Reports -> Manage Accounts Receivable -> A/R Aging Summary

- Notice the columns showing the customers' timeliness and overall balances

- Review Sales

Review Sales reports allow you to figure out how well are you doing by analyzing sales and discovering where you make your money the most. This report includes but is not limited to sales by customer summary, sales by product and/or services summary, as well as income by customer summary, list of customer contacts, and more. Business owners need to have visibility into the best (and worst) products so they know what to sell more of. They also need visibility into the customer by

Reporting

customer activity so they can market and/or reward the most valuable customers.

Customer Sales Summary a.k.a. "How much has each customer purchased from me?"

The Sales by Customer Summary report can be very valuable as you see those customers who contribute the most to the success of your company. It is considering the sales transactions for each customer for the period specified.

Step by Step: Sales by Customer Summary

1. Reports -> All Reports -> Review Sales -> Sales by Customer Summary.

2. Customize -> Date: All Dates -> Sort by Total in descending order.

3. Notice the top customers who have purchased product and/or services over time.

Customer Detail sales a.k.a. "What are the detailed sales by the customer?"

This report is a more detailed version of Sales by Customer Summary. In addition to income from each customer, this report includes all transactions that contributed to each total. Set the dates on this report to give you a complete history of what transpired with your customers over that timeframe.

Step by Step: Sales by Customer Detail

Reports -> All Reports -> Review Sales -> Sales by Customer Detail.

Date: Custom From MM/DD/YYYY To MM/DD/YYYY

Notice the columns showing Date, Product/Service, QTY, Rate and Balance.

Product/Service Detail Summary a.k.a. "What are the detailed sales by product or service?"

This report is a more detailed version of Sales by Product/Service Summary. In addition to the unit and dollar sales for each product or service, this report lists the transactions that contributed to each total. See which products/services were the most popular or made the most sales during the timeframe you specify.

Step by Step: Sales by Product/Service Detail

Reports -> All Reports ->Review Sales -> Sales by Product/Service Detail.

Date: Last Quarter.

Notice the columns showing Date, Product/Service, Customer, QTY, Rate and Balance

Unbilled Charges Report a.k.a. "What charges do I need to create invoices for?"

This report lists transactions that were marked billable to a customer when the expense was entered, but they have not yet appeared on an invoice. For example, an IT company was helping a client with a new network setup. They needed to purchase a server on behalf of the client in order to continue with the job. The client now owes them reimbursement for that server. If they mark Billable on the credit card charge that bought the server and enter the client in the Customer field, then the server will show up on the Unbilled Charges report until the invoice is created.

Step by Step: Unbilled Charges

- Select Global Create -> Delayed Charge (you may need to click Show More).

- From the Customer dropdown, select the vendor or customer in question.

- From the Product/Service dropdown, select Design. The description, QTY, Rate and Amount will pre-fill.

- Click Save and Close.

- Reports -> All Reports -> Review Sales -> Unbilled Charges.

Manage Accounts Payable

Accounts Payable managing reports allow you to see what you owe to your vendors and at what time you're obliged to pay them, so you can make use of the breathing space, but also to be prepared to pay your dues. The reports include: A/P Aging Summary and Detail, Vendor Balance Summary and Detail, Bill Payment List, Unpaid Bills. As a business owner, managing cash going out of the business is crucial. Weighing whether to pay something early, on time, or late can only be considered if one knows what is upcoming by running these reports.

A/P Aging Summary a.k.a. "How much do I owe to each vendor, and how much is overdue?"

This report summarizes the status of unpaid bills and unapplied vendor credits. This report serves as a quick glance for seeing which vendors you are the furthest overdue on. When cash comes in, use this report to pay vendors strategically instead of just paying the first ones you come to. If you owe a vendor that is charging you finance charges, then you don't want to pay a different vendor's bill that is still current (unless other factors influence that decision) when you could pay down the bill, you're getting charged interest on. For each vendor that is owed money, the report shows: Total bills that have been entered but unpaid in the current period Totals owed to the vendors from previous periods.

Step by Step: A/P Aging Summary

Reports -> All Reports -> Manage Accounts Payable -> A/P Aging Summary.

Notice the columns showing Vendors, Current, Past Due by days late, and Totals.

Vendor Balance Detail a.k.a. "What's the detail behind what I owe to vendors?"

The vendor balance report lists the vendors to whom you owe money and how long ago since the bill was due. This report shows the unpaid vendor balances. It can be very important information for a business owner to have, but it is useful to others as well. For example, your company's bank may want to review your vendor balance report if you are looking for a loan. If a vendor shows on this report, then that indicates there are open transactions that need to be paid or applied. This report gives you each instance where that is the case. Click through to see the detail behind the transaction.

Review Expenses And Purchases

Review Expenses and Purchases reports allow you to see where you're spending your money. The reports include: Expenses by Vendor Summary, Transaction List by Vendor, Vendor Contact List, Open Purchase Order List, Purchases by Vendor Detail, and Purchases by Product/Service Detail. Business owners focus a lot of time and energy to evaluate how they can control and cut down on costs. Use these reports to facilitate a better flow of information for more effective decision making.

Transaction List by Vendor a.k.a. "What have my interactions been with each of my vendors?"

The Transaction List by Vendor report will list all interactions with each vendor during the date range specified. Transactions can include Cash Expenses, Credit Card Expenses, Bills, Bill Payments, Checks, and even Purchase Orders. This report could be compared against a monthly transaction statement provided by the vendor to ensure all entries on both sets of books match up exactly. Any discrepancies can be identified and addressed with the vendor.

Activity: Transaction List by Vendor

- Reports -> All Reports -> Review Expenses and Purchases -> Transaction List by Vendor.

- Notice the easy-to-follow layout, transaction type, memos, and amounts.

- Vendor Contact List a.k.a. "Where can I print off a list of my vendors and their contact information?"

- The Vendor Contact List shows you a list of vendors with any contact info you have for each of those vendors. If you have additional info to add or if something needs to be changed, then you can click on the vendor's name and the Vendor setup screen pops up for you to edit the info. Upon saving, you'll need to refresh the browser so that the report is updated.

- Activity: Vendor Balance Detail

- Reports -> All Reports -> Manage Accounts Payable -> Vendor Balance Detail.

- Notice the columns showing Vendors, Dates, Amounts and Balances.

Manage Payroll

Manage Employees reports help you see the employee activities and payroll. Whether you have payroll turned on or not, the reports include: Time Activities by Employee Detail and Recent/Edited Time Activities. Business owners use the time reports to monitor the employee activity and ensure timely entry of data. This group becomes Manage Payroll if you have the payroll module turned on inside of QuickBooks Online.

Manage Sales Tax

Manage Sales Tax reports allow you to manage the sales taxes you have collected and then report and pay the appropriate tax agencies. The reports include: Taxable Sales Summary and Detail, Sales Tax Liability Report. All business owners must be aware of the potential for sales tax collection and payment in the place of business and as they deal with other locations. Based on the details entered in QuickBooks, Sales tax reports help to prepare monthly, quarterly, or annual sales tax returns.

Sales Tax Liability Report a.k.a. "What did I collect in sales tax last quarter?"

The Sales Tax Liability Report lists each government entity and sales tax rate you have charged to your customers for the time period specified. Print this report to help with sales tax filings. For more information, click on the Sales Tax center and see the Gross sales versus Taxable sales to find out the amounts of exempt (non-taxable) sales, which often need to be reported alongside what sales tax was collected.

Products And Inventory Managing

Products and Inventory managing reports are useful for understanding not only exactly how much inventory you possess, as well as how much you pay for and make on each of the items in the inventory. The reports include: Inventory Valuation Summary and Detail, Product/Service purchases, Sales by Product/Services Summary and Detail. Business Owners are required to maintain accurate on-hand inventory records. For basic inventory tracking, QuickBooks Online provides the reports needed to track the inventory and have visibility into purchases and sales of those products.

Inventory Valuation Summary a.k.a. "How much inventory do I have on hand?"

The Inventory Valuation Summary shows you how much quantity of each product you have as well as how much you've paid in total for those quantities, resulting in an average cost per product. The total asset value should match the Balance Sheet inventory balance as of the same date.

Deposit Detail a.k.a. "What individual customer payments make up each deposit?"

The Deposit Detail report can help you identify missing or incorrect info regarding the bank deposits. When looking at this report, compare each line item to the deposit slip itself and make sure that any customer payments received are booked as such instead of as additional income.

Trial Balance a.k.a. "What is the debit versus credit balances in all of my accounts?"

As of the specified date, the Trial Balance lists all accounts in the chart of accounts with their associated debit or credit balance on that date. Total debits will always equal total credits

Recent Automatic Transactions a.k.a. "What transactions were automatically added from my recurring transaction list?"

Often, we'll set up recurring transactions to be automatically entered on a certain date. This report allows us to see which ones were automatically entered within the last 4 days. For instance, you set 10 recurring transactions to automatically enter on the 1st of each month. This report should get run on the 2nd or 3rd of each month to capture those automatic transactions.

Journal "What actually happened behind the scenes with debits and credits this month?" The Journal report shows each transaction's debits and credits during the specified time and displays them chronologically. It is a great backup support when documenting the detail of the month or quarter for a tax return, audit, or other financial statements.

List Reports There are a few different ways to pull a list report in QuickBooks Online. First, we click on the Gear icon, and under the List column, you can see a shortcut for the Products and Services list and the Recurring Transactions list. If we click on All Lists, we can see the option to access many different lists:

Step by Step: To run a Customer List

- Open the Report Dashboard/Center.
- Click the All Reports grouping.
- Click on Review Sales.
- Scroll down to the Customer Contact List.

Step by Step: For Vendors

- Start with the All Reports grouping.

- Click on Review Expenses and Purchases.

- You can choose to print the Vendor Contact List.

- Open the Report Dashboard/Center.

- Click the All Reports grouping.

- Click on Vendors and Purchases.

- Scroll down to the Customer Contact List.

- My Custom Reports

After you have performed all the customizing and filtering required to create a more useful report for yourself or your client, saving those customizations saves you time for every future time you need to run the same report. You can decide whether you want to be the only one to see the report or if you want all users to be able to see the report (subject to the user permissions they have set up).

Activity: Custom Reports

- Find and display the report you want to customize. To change what's in the report click on the Customize option.

- Mark the box to add a Subcolumn for Year-To-Date. Click Run Report.

- Once the report is customized the way you like it, click Save Customizations.

- Enter a descriptive name for the report in the Name of the custom report: field.

- Click share this report with all company users. If you do not select it, then this custom report is available only to your user.

- Click OK

Heads-up: Adding reports to a group allows you to set a common email schedule for all the reports in the group. The reports appear under the group name on your list of custom reports. If you add a report with an email schedule to a group that also has an email schedule, the newly added report will follow the group's email schedule. Once you Save Customizations of a report or group of reports, select Reports -> My Custom Reports to then run, export to Excel, edit or delete them from this list. You'll see a list of all custom or groups of custom reports. Select the report or group of reports you want and click on the function in the top

Reporting

right. You can also set a schedule for automatically sending the report (by itself or with a group of other reports) by email either in HTML format (it looks like the website in the email) or in Excel format.

You can have standard reports sent to you that will help you monitor information. You can have standard financial reports sent or weekly sales reports sent to you. If you have a standard set of reports that need to be sent, there may be zero customization required on some of them but running the standard reports once and memorizing them into a group to get sent together will provide useful automation. Side note: If you change the settings on a custom report, you need to click Save Customizations again to save the changes.

Activity: Automatic Distribution

- Reports -> My Custom Reports.

- Click on the report or report group you desire. Click Edit.

- Click the box next to Set the email schedule for this report. More options will appear.

- Click Edit Schedule to set the desired timeframes (Weekly).

- Enter the email information (separate multiple email addresses with a comma or semicolon).

- Enter a subject line and standard Note to be attached.

- Select the method of delivery (default is HTML in the body of the email). Click Save.

- Heads-up: One helpful use of the automatic distribution report is to select "problem" accounts that you often receive phone calls about. Customize a report and set the automatic distribution to email you the detail of this account on a weekly or monthly basis so that you know when something needs your attention. This allows you to be proactive when you notice a build-up of issues that need to be addressed.

- Export Reports

- You can export reports in QuickBooks Online by downloading the report in Excel format. This can be helpful for sending, modifying, printing, and analyzing data. To export a report, follow these easy steps:

- Open the report that you would like to export.

- Click the blue Excel button from the top toolbar in the report.

- The report will download as an Excel file to your default downloads folder.

- Send Reports

- Sending reports from QuickBooks Online is a quick and easy way to share financial information. The default format for sending reports is as in-line HTML. You can send reports to multiple recipients and even include a note in your email. Follow these steps to send a report:

- Open the report that you would like to send.

- Click the blue Email button from the top toolbar in the report.

- Type in the email address you wish to send to.

- Add a note if you wish.

- Press Send.

Cash Flow Statement

Thanks to non-cash accounting anomalies like accrual reporting and depreciation, Profit & Loss reports don't tell you what you've got in your proverbial wallet. Looking at your cash flow statement report helps you figure out whether your company generates enough cash to keep the doors open. Your balance sheet might look great—$10 million in assets and only $500,000 in liabilities, say—but if a $50,000 payment is due and you have only $3,000 in the bank, you have cash flow problems. The concept of cash flow is easy to understand. It's just as every film-noir detective says, follow the money. Cash flow is nothing more than the real money that flows into and out of your company—

not the noncash transactions, such as depreciation, that you see on a Profit & Loss report.

Making a cash flow statement is easy because you have only one report to choose from. Simply choose Reports→Company & Financial→Statement of Cash Flows, and QuickBooks creates a report that displays your cash flow for your fiscal year to date. To look at your cash flow report for a quarter or a prolonged period, in the Dates box, choose This Fiscal Quarter or This Fiscal Year.

Accounts Receivable and Payable Aging Report

In between performing work, invoicing customers, and collecting payments, you have to keep track of what amount is owed by which customer (known as Accounts Receivable) and when the money is due. Sure, you can tack on finance charges to light a fire under your customers' accounting departments, but such charges are rarely enough to make up for the time and effort you spend collecting overdue payments. Far preferable are customers who pay on time without reminders, gentle or otherwise. Because companies need money to keep things running, you'll have to spend some time keeping track of your Accounts Receivable and the payments that come in. In this chapter, you'll learn the ins and outs of tracking what customers owe, receiving payments from them, and dinging them if they don't pay on time. You'll get up to speed on Income Tracker (new in QuickBooks 2014), a handy dashboard that shows estimates you've created, how much customers owe—both overdue and not—and what's been paid in the past 30 days. QuickBooks' Collections Center can highlight customers with overdue or almost-due invoices, gather the info you need to collect what customers owe, and make it easy to send out reminders. In contrast to invoices, sales receipts are the simplest and most immediate sales forms in QuickBooks. When your customers pay in full at the time of the sale—at your retail store, for example—you can create a sale's receipt, so the customer has a record of the purchase and payment. At the same time, QuickBooks posts the money from the sale into your bank account (in QuickBooks, anyway) or the Undeposited Funds account. (Sales receipts work only when customers pay in full, because that type of sales form can't handle previous customer payments and balances.) In this chapter, you'll learn how to create sales receipts for one sale at a time and to summarize a day's worth of merchandising.

Conclusion

Thousands of small companies and nonprofit organizations turn to QuickBooks to keep their finances on track. And over the years, Intuit has introduced various editions of the program to satisfy the needs of different types of companies. Back when milk was simply milk, you either used QuickBooks or you didn't. But now, when you can choose milk from soybeans and rice as well as cows—and with five different levels of fat—it's no surprise that QuickBooks comes in a variety of editions (which, in some cases, are dramatically different from their siblings), as well as six industry-specific editions.

Choosing which QuickBooks installation to use can be difficult, luckily, we've dedicated this portion of the book exactly to that. The six industry specific editions will ensure that you're not paying a dime over what you need for the privilege to use QuickBooks.

From the smallest of sole proprietorships to burgeoning enterprises, one of these editions is likely to meet your organization's needs and budget. QuickBooks isn't hard to learn, as you've seen so far.

Many of the features that you're familiar with from other programs work the same way in QuickBooks—windows, dialog boxes, dropdown lists, and keyboard shortcuts, to name a few. And with each new version, Intuit has added enhancements and features to make your workflow smoother and faster. The challenge is knowing what to do according to accounting rules, and how to do it in QuickBooks. This book teaches you how to use QuickBooks and explains the accounting concepts behind what you're doing.

When you hear "small-business accounting software," you probably think of QuickBooks. Since Intuit launched its flagship product over 20 years ago, the financial management platform has dominated the accounting software marketplace. Since then, it has been steadily improving. Inuit launches excellent, feature-packed updates relatively often, ensuring that you get the best experience possible.

Currently, QuickBooks software holds more than 80 percent of the small-business market share. If you're researching small-business accounting solutions, clearly QuickBooks will be on your list.

But exactly which version suits you best? On-premise or cloud? With payroll or without?

QuickBooks has a product for nearly all your accounting needs but sorting through the options can feel like an insurmountable task.

QuickBooks Self-Employed

- The newest edition of the QuickBooks product line is a cloud-based financial management service designed for self-employed and/or freelance individuals (e.g., anyone who contracts out their services, such as an Uber driver)
- The solution comes in two packages: Self-Employed and Self-Employed Tax Bundle.
- QuickBooks Self-Employed allows users to:
- Connect to bank and credit card accounts
- Track income and expenses, separating transactions as business or personal
- Categorize and track IRS Schedule C tax deductions and expenses
- Calculate quarterly taxes

Conclusion

- QuickBooks Self-Employed Tax Bundle offers the same functionality as Self-Employed with a connection to Intuit TurboTax, allowing users to:

- Pay quarterly taxes online

- Export Schedule C deductions to TurboTax

QuickBooks Online

In 2014, Intuit reported a major turning point for QuickBooks products: For the first time, more new customers chose QuickBooks Online over desktop versions.

Since then, QuickBooks Online has grown to over 1 million subscribers, signaling that small businesses are growing more confident hosting their accounting solutions in the cloud.

QuickBooks' cloud-based solution is designed for small-business users and comes in three packages: Simple Start, Essentials and Plus.

QuickBooks Online Products: Common Capabilities

- -Accounts payable and accounts receivable

- -Monitor and manage income and expenses.

- -Billing and invoicing

- -Send unlimited estimates and invoices

- -Essentials and Plus also offer recurring invoices.

- -Expense management

- -Track and process work-related expenses such as travel and supplies.

- -Financial reporting

- -Simple Start has over 20 pre-built reports, Essentials has over 40 and Plus has over 60 (includes sales and tax reports).

- The QuickBooks Simple Start package includes:

- One user license

- Data import from Excel or QuickBooks desktop versions

- Access for up to two accounting professionals (accountant and/or bookkeeper)

- QuickBooks Essentials includes the above capabilities as well as:

- Three user licenses

- Ability to set user permissions (accountant, bookkeeper, etc.)

- Ability to postdate bills and payments

- QuickBooks Plus includes all the above and more. Additional offerings include:

- Five user licenses

- Inventory tracking

- Creating and sending purchase orders

QuickBooks Desktop Products

It's important to note while QuickBooks Online will be the best choice for many small businesses due to the ease of use and access, the online version is not identical to the desktop products.

They offer similar capabilities, but the breadth and depth of the features differ. For example, the most report options included online is about 60—with QuickBooks Online Plus—while the desktop products start at 100 with industry-specific options available.

There are several QuickBooks products under the Desktop umbrella. In this article, we are discussing the 2016 version of each. They include:

- -Mac: Designed for small businesses using Apple OS (not scalable).

- -Pro: A great idea for fresh small businesses, those who've just begun (can scale to Premier and Enterprise).

- -Premier: Aimed at small businesses with industry-specific needs (can scale to Enterprise)

- -Enterprise: Designed for small to midsize businesses (SMBs) that need a flexible business and financial management solution.

The desktop products have a similar base feature set, with functionalities becoming more advanced as the scale of the package.

QuickBooks Desktop Products: Common Capabilities:

- Core accounting

- Managing accounts receivable/payable, general books and bank reconciliation.

- Payroll (limited)

- Track employee hours and print checks and deposit slips. Enhanced payroll is available for an additional fee (calculates payroll taxes and files tax forms).

- Billing and invoicing

- Automates creating and sending invoices as well as payment collection.

- Inventory management

Conclusion

- Tracks orders, sales, and deliveries to maintain product supply levels.

- Financial reporting

- Tracks and visualizes trends, evaluates KPI and profitability, such as profit and loss (P&L) statements, balance sheets, etc.

QuickBooks Mac Desktop

Businesses should note; however—QuickBooks' Mac desktop product is not scalable, whereas the Windows versions of Pro, Premier and Enterprise are.

In addition to the common desktop capabilities listed above, Mac Desktop includes:

The "Income Tracker" dashboard, which displays unpaid invoices

Project accounting to invoice for projects in phases

Budget management to create fiscal year budgets and track progress

QuickBooks Pro

QuickBooks Pro is designed for small businesses that are just getting started. It's simple enough for business owners that lack advanced accounting knowledge and makes it easy for them to share files and data with their accountant.

Pro allows up to three users to work within QuickBooks at the same time (requires separate user licenses). The Pro package offers the common capabilities listed in the table above, plus the following:

The "Bill Tracker" dashboard lets users see unpaid bills, purchase orders, etc. all in one place

Tracks sales and expenses in multiple currencies

Easy data import from Excel, Quicken and older QuickBooks versions

QuickBooks Premiere

QuickBooks Premier targets small business users that have industry-specific needs. It is especially beneficial for those in industries such as non-profit, retail, professional services, contractors and manufacturing.

QuickBooks Premiere is ideal for those that are just starting out in the entrepreneurship world. If you have your goals set and are ready to dip into the world of business full-force, then QuickBooks Premiere is for you.

Premier supports more concurrent users than Pro or Mac: Up to five users can work in QuickBooks Premier at the same time (requires separate user licenses).

Premier has all the features of Pro, as well as:

Job costing and estimating

Budgeting and forecasting

Industry-specific reports (including the ability to run a P&L by job or client)

QuickBooks Enterprise

QuickBooks Enterprise is Intuit's most comprehensive business and financial management solution because it includes several applications, such as QuickBooks Payroll (see QuickBooks Apps below). Enterprise is designed for both small and midsized businesses, supporting up to 30 user licenses.

Enterprise is sold in three packages: Silver, Gold, and Platinum. Each Enterprise package includes the same capabilities as the Pro and Premier packages along with several others, including:

Up to 14 predefined user roles (admin, accountant, etc.)

Multiple users can access files at the same time

"Expanded list" allows businesses to track over 100,000 employees, customers, vendors and inventory items (Pro and Premier allow 14,500)

Quickbooks Apps

Intuit has several branded applications designed to enhance the functionality of the above-mentioned platforms. Businesses can purchase these add-ons for an additional fee:

QuickBooks Payments: Allows businesses to email invoices and accept payments online via credit card or ACH transfers.

QuickBooks POS: A cloud-based, iPad point-of-sale (POS) system. Allows businesses to ring up sales, accept credit cards and keep track of inventory from the POS dashboard.

QuickBooks Payroll: Allows businesses to pay up to 50 employees by check or direct deposit. Automatically calculates state and federal tax and files year-end W-2 tax forms.

QuickBooks has established itself as a major player in the small to midsize business accounting market. Whether you're just starting out, or you're expanding and have more advanced accounting needs, QuickBooks has a solution designed to fit your business.

Frequently Asked Questions

How do I register my copy of Enterprise Solutions?

You can register online or by phone. Go to the Help menu and click Register QuickBooks.

How do I contact technical support?

Go to the QuickBooks Support Site at www.quickbooks.com/support.

How do I purchase additional user licenses?

You can add users to your QuickBooks Enterprise Solutions in two ways: „ Purchase additional copies of QuickBooks Enterprise Solutions in a store. „ Buy additional user licenses by phone or web. To add a license by phone or web, go to the Help menu, click Manage My License, and then click Buy additional user license. Follow the onscreen instructions.

How do I move my company file from one computer to another?

To move company files from one computer to another, QuickBooks recommends using a portable file provider. The portable company file does not simply copy the data for your company; it compresses the data into a smaller file.

To move your company file:

Make the company portable file:

Go to the File menu and click the option which you want to do.

Click Portable company file and then click Next.

Select the drive (hard drive, CD, or ZIP disk) where you want to save the portable company file.

Click Save.

Take the media containing your portable company file to the computer to which you want to move your company file.

Open the portable company file on the destination computer: a Go to the File menu and click Open or Restore Company.

Click Restore a portable file and click Next.

Browse to select the portable company file you want to restore, click Open, and then click Next.

Browse to select and change the location and file name associated with the file you want to be created and opened from the portable company file. If you select an existing company file, it will be overwritten with the data from the portable company file.

Click Save

How do I remove older or unneeded transactions from my data file?

The Clean Up Company Data utility exists to remove transactions for which you no longer need to keep detailed records. You can choose to remove transactions from a specific date (for example, all transactions date on or before 12/31/04). Optionally, you can choose to remove unused list items, such as obsolete customers and items. Before removing the transactions, Enterprise Solutions makes a copy of your company's file that is archived and enters general journal transactions that summarize the transactions being removed. To remove older or unneeded transactions:

Go to the File menu, click Utilities, and then click Clean Up Company Data.

Select one of the options:

To remove transactions from a specific date, select Remove transactions from a specific date and then select the date from the date box.

To remove all transactions in the file, click Remove ALL transactions.

Click Next and follow the onscreen instructions.

How do I download and install an update or patch?

Periodically, Intuit provides updates to QuickBooks Enterprise Solutions that you can download from the Internet. These updates can include a maintenance release (also known as a patch), a new feature, a new service, or timely information that could be relevant to your business. In order to update QuickBooks, access the help menu and click Update QuickBooks. Follow the onscreen instructions. If you store your company file on a file server and installed the Enterprise Solutions application on that server, you need to periodically run Enterprise Solutions on the server and apply patches and updates.

How do I back up or restore my company file?

Back up your company files daily. Backup copies are important insurance; if you should lose data for any reason, you can restore data from your backup copy. Enterprise Solutions enables you to back up and restore your data in several ways. To back up a company file:

Go to the File menu and click what you want to do with it.

Choose the backup option you want, click Next, and follow the onscreen instructions.

To restore a company file:

Go to the File menu and select Open or Restore Company.

Choose the restore option you want, click Next, and follow the onscreen instructions. To view detailed instructions for each backup and restore option, refer to the in-product Help.

What should I do if I forget my password?

QuickBooks 2004 and later releases support case-sensitive passwords. If you believe you are entering the correct password but still get the message "The password you typed is incorrect," your password might include mixed-cased characters. Try the following solutions: Enter Admin and then click OK without typing a password. Enter your password with Caps Lock or Num Lock turned on or off. Enter variations of your password, using mixed upper- and lower-case characters. Enter the password with a space before or after the actual password. Enter the password in a text editor, such as WordPad or Notepad, to confirm that your keyboard is functioning properly. Restore a pre-update backup of your file that does not have the case-sensitive password. When you restore this file, you can set your new administrator password at the end of the update process. If you are still unable to access your file, go to the Password Recovery website: www.quickbooks.com/removepassword (additional fees may apply).

How do I update my payroll to use the latest tax tables?

If you are a QuickBooks Payroll subscriber, you have two options for updating your tax tables: Go to the Employees menu, click Get Payroll Updates, and then click Update. Turn on the

Auto-update preference. When a new tax table is available, it is downloaded automatically, and you are prompted to install. Payroll updates, which might include compliance enhancements and updated payroll tax forms as well as new tax tables, become available throughout the year. We recommend that you connect to the payroll service at least every 45 days to make sure you have the most current tax table available. Make sure that you download and install the latest payroll update before you pay employees for the first time.

How do I add another company's EIN to existing Payroll subscription?

To add an EIN for another company:

Go to the File menu and select Open/Restore Company. Select Open a company file, select Next. Choose the company file you want to add and click Open.

Go to the Employees menu, click Payroll Service Activities, and then click Use my existing Payroll subscription. When asked if you want help setting up payroll, click Yes.

Click Add To Subscription and click Next.

Enter and confirm the new EIN to be associated with your existing subscription.

Click Done. Enterprise Solutions updates your subscription in the new company file. You can run payroll immediately. Note

Conclusion

QuickBooks Standard and Enhanced payroll subscriptions can process payroll for up to three businesses (EINs) on the same payroll subscription. QuickBooks Enhanced Payroll for Accountants can process payroll for up to 50 EINs on the same payroll subscription.

Key Shortcuts

- -To start QuickBooks without a company file press Ctrl (while opening)

- -To suppress the desktop windows (in the Open Company window) press Alt (while opening)

- -Display product information about your software version press F2

- -Close active window press Esc or Ctrl + F4

- -Dates Key Next day + (plus key)

- -Previous day - (minus key)

- -Today T

- -First day of the week W

- -Last day of the week K

- -First day of the month M

- -Last day of the month H

A Comprehensive Guide To Quickbooks

- -First day of the year Y
- -Last day of the year R
- -Date calendar Alt + (down arrow)
- Edit transaction selected in register or lift Ctrl + E
- -Delete character to the right of insertion point Del
- -Delete character to the left of insertion point Backspace
- -Delete line from detail area Ctrl + Del
- -Insert line in detail area Ctrl + Ins
- -Cut selected characters Ctrl + X
- -Copy selected characters Ctrl + C
- -Paste cut or copied characters Ctrl + V
- -Increase check or another form number by one + (plus key)
- -Decrease check or another form number by one - (minus key)
- -Undo changes made in field Ctrl + Z
- -Help Windows Key
- -Display Help in context F1

- -Go to next Help topic Tab
- -Go to previous Help topic Shift + Tab
- -Display selected topic Enter

References

Biafore, B. (2008). QuickBooks 2008: The Missing Manual. Sebastopol, CA: O'Reilly Media.

Nelson, S. L. (2018). *QuickBooks 2018 For Dummies*. Hoboken, NJ: John Wiley & Sons.

Sleeter Group, I. (2006). *Learning QuickBooks Step-by-Step - QuickBooks Fundamentals - Version 2006*. The Sleeter Group.

Made in the USA
Monee, IL
30 January 2020